Praise for *Coaching Through Burnout*

"The modern workplace is facing a mental health crisis which includes rising cases of burnout. This book is an invaluable and practical guide, an essential manual for leaders, managers and team members. Not only does it support the development of effective coaching skills, it applies the evidence based processes from ACT in an accessible and practical way. Hazel brings her unique voice, humanity, experience and deep expertise to this book. The stories she shares are relatable and powerful and will help leaders tackle what can be uncomfortable conversations in an effective and impactful way."

> Ross McIntosh – Business Psychologist, Coach and Host of the *People Soup* Podcast

"Hazel has long been a person able to weave technical knowledge and personal experiences to support others in their journey. Her ability to make the nonsensical to us make perfect sense is incredible. This book has facts, supportive advice, personal experiences and well needed humour to create a beautiful mesh of support for those experiencing burnout or wanting to know more about it. It's a must have for your bookshelf at home, but equally for organisations and professionals looking at their approaches to burnout support."

> Daniel Winter-Bates, Head of Inclusion and Sustainability, NHS Hampshire and Isle of Wight Integrated Care Board

"This is a brilliant book, and an important resource for coaches, managers and team members. While many of us spent the pandemic in limbo, waiting for the economy to open up again, Hazel was in the trenches, working with NHS leaders to support them in an incredibly challenging environment. Burnout is something that, as the saying goes, happens gradually, then suddenly. Hazel has taken her learnings from the NHS to create a coaching framework that helps people, whatever their circumstances at work. And as a dedicated Acceptance and Commitment Coach, she offers great insights into a model that allows coaches at any stage in their journey to significantly deepen their practice."

Jim Godfrey, Executive Coach (PCC, CPCC).
Former Communications Leader (ITV, Starbucks,
Jawbone) and UK Government Special Adviser

"I have been coaching across global organisations for more than 20 years, and I think every one of my clients would appreciate Hazel's book. A clear, evidence-based, and practical guide to showing up in your own work life, taking action based on your values and looking after yourself. No waffle, no ego, just concrete psychologically sound advice that makes a difference. I'll be recommending it to all my future clients."

Liz Margree, Coaching and Business Psychologist,
Director of Liz Margree & Associates Ltd.

"It's so refreshing to read a book that isn't about the latest fad from a self-appointed 'expert' who doesn't understand the demands we face. This book is down-to-earth, practical and frankly invaluable."

Nikki Richards, Deputy Chief Executive,
Royal Berkshire Fire & Rescue Service, UK.

"*Coaching Through Burnout* will transform the way you relate to and coach those who are navigating the many layers of burnout. The mix of storytelling, personal insights, exploration of concepts, and practical tools for execution will leave you with an empowered path forward to walk people through freedom from one of our modern lives' biggest hindrances. This book is a non-negotiable for anyone looking to be an informed coach in this area."

Megan Monahan, Meditation teacher and author of *Don't Hate, Meditate*

"I commissioned Hazel to support the NHS with coaching during Covid. Distilled in this book you will find practical wisdom that comes from supporting people to be at their most resourceful and perform well in the most challenging times. A must read for all of us striving to be at our best for ourselves and our teams."

Helen Ives, Chief People Officer, NHS Professionals

COACHING
THROUGH
BURNOUT

A burnout prevention toolkit for busy leaders and their teams

Hazel Anderson-Turner

Copyright © 2025 by Hazel Anderson-Turner

All rights reserved. No part of this publication may be reproduced, distributed or transmitted in anyform or by any means without permission of the publisher, except in the case of brief quotations referencing the body of work and in accordance with copyright law.

The information given in this book should not be treated as a substitute for professional medical advice; always consult a medical practitioner. Any use of information in this book is at the reader's discretion and risk. Neither the author nor the publisher can be held responsible for any loss, claim or damage arising out of the use, or misuse, of the suggestions made, the failure to take medical advice of for any material on third party websites.

ISBN 978-1-916529-38-0 Paperback
ISBN 978-1-916529-39-7 Ebook

The Unbound Press
www.theunboundpress.com

Hey unbound one!

Welcome to this magical book brought to you by
The Unbound Press.

At The Unbound Press we believe that when women write freely from the fullest expression of who they are, it can't help but activate a feeling of deep connection and transformation in others. When we come together, we become more and we're changing the world, one book at a time!

This book has been carefully crafted by both the author and publisher with the intention of inspiring you to move ever more deeply into who you truly are.

We hope that this book helps you to connect with your Unbound Self and that you feel called to pass it on to others who want to live a more fully expressed life.

With much love,
Nicola Humber

Founder of The Unbound Press

www.theunboundpress.com

This book is dedicated to everyone I have coached and taught in the NHS and Emergency Services over the last five years. It wouldn't feel right to start this book without saying thank you for everything you did during the Covid Pandemic, and continue to do.

It's also for my daughter, Indie, and partner, Steve, who together have shown me what love really is.

Contents

Foreword	xiii
Part 1: The Why and the What	**1**
Introduction	3
1. What is Burnout?	17
Part 2: How Conversations Can Help Prevent Burnout	**31**
2. The Power of Conversation	33
3. Do I Have Your Full Attention?	45
4. Conversation Traps	57
5. Asking Useful Questions	71
6. Structuring Our Questions	83
7. Starting a Wellbeing Conversation	91
8. Gavin's Story	107
Part 3: How Psychological Flexibility Can Help Prevent Burnout	**111**
9. Let's Get Flexible	113
10. Waking Up a Frog	127
11. What Matters Most?	143
12. Befriending Our Inner Critic	159
Final Words	177
Acknowledgements	181
Abbreviations	183
References	185
Resources	189
Further Reading	191
About the Author	195

Foreword

During the pandemic in 2020, I came closer to experiencing burnout than ever before. My private practice as a clinical psychologist saw an overwhelming influx of clients desperate for help as they navigated the complexities of lockdown. Simultaneously, like many of us, I had to transition to working online from home. This included moving our training company fully online, while at the same time, adapting our national university postgraduate programs to remote teaching. Amidst this whirlwind, I was also managing the challenges of home working and parenting.

Twelve months in, I felt completely frazzled—constantly tired, overwhelmed, and utterly disconnected from my work. To top it off, I could see I wasn't using the very strategies I taught others every day! It was like being a chef who burns their own dinner—how does that happen?

After a particularly challenging day, where I forgot two client meetings, missed a major deadline, and was late to pick up the kids from school, I realised I probably needed to make a few changes in my life.

I gradually began a process of slowing down and moving out of autopilot mode. I built a habit of catching (and not always listening to) my critical inner voice that insisted I had to work harder, faster, and better at all times. Crucially, I started to say no to things that weren't on my priority list and yes to what truly mattered. Gradually, these actions helped me develop a healthier relationship with my work and my wellbeing returned.

This journey through burnout has allowed me to appreciate the profound value of Hazel Anderson-Turner's work. The book you hold in your hands serves as a much-needed resource for those helping individuals facing similar challenges. It offers a practical and compassionate approach to navigating the complex interplay of personal experiences and external pressures that contribute to burnout.

Filled with the author's wisdom and coaching expertise, this book provides practical examples of how Hazel has successfully guided individuals through their own burnout journeys. You'll discover tools that make a real difference in people's lives and gain insight into her humane and respectful stance. Together, these elements create a powerful approach to addressing this important issue.

Having known Hazel Anderson-Turner for over ten years, I have witnessed first-hand the depth she brings to her work. One noticeable quality is her vulnerability and openness; she shares her personal experiences in a way that helps others grasp and apply these concepts in their own lives. Her creativity and humour provide a rich backdrop for this book.

This manual sharpens and hones your skills to assist individuals experiencing burnout. It will help you become a better listener, ensuring that those sitting across from you feel heard and validated—an essential foundation for effective work. Hazel describes how Acceptance and Commitment Therapy (ACT) provides clear, evidence-based tools that help clients move beyond habitual responses to burnout, fostering mindful awareness and reducing excessive self-criticism. These tools create a context for individuals to reflect on what truly matters in their lives—questions that are often too difficult to answer when overwhelmed by burnout.

Overall, this book offers practical tools and strategies to prevent burnout in yourself and others. Importantly, Hazel suggests a stance that is deeply respectful and validating, while remaining optimistic and hopeful for the future.

I am grateful to Hazel for writing this book, as I know it will be immensely beneficial for you as a reader and, if you are a coach, for the individuals you work with.

Good luck on your journey with this book!

Dr Joe Oliver
Consultant Clinical Psychologist/Associate Professor
Founder of Contextual Consulting and co-author of
ACTivate Your Life (2nd ed).

PART 1

The Why and the What

Introduction

"Will the book sound like you?" Gavin asked. You'll meet Gavin, a wonderful man, and one of my very first *Coaching Through Burnout* delegates, in Chapter Eight. "I guess what I mean is that I really hope your energy and enthusiasm for the topic, and how genuine you are, will come across in the book. That's the thing that really made a difference to me when I attended your course."

I hope that I've achieved what Gavin was looking for. This is not an academic book. Yes, I share insights and research, but essentially this is a book about practical skills and stories. Stories, which when pieced together, tell a bigger narrative about how we can navigate being human in this complex, confusing, and often exhausting, modern world.

I was inspired to write this book after coaching and training hundreds of incredible National Health Service

(NHS) staff through a very challenging period in our history, the Covid pandemic. In this book I will share tools and techniques that have helped my clients to feel better equipped to deal with the physical, cognitive and emotional demands they faced day after day.

One of the things I learnt about burnout is how important it is to act early. Once exhaustion and disengagement set in, sickness rates understandably rise, increasing the level of demand placed on other team members and the team leader, who then are at greater risk of burning out themselves. Burnout is not something that we can hope will go away on its own. This is why preventative action and early intervention is so important. I hope this book supports more people to have the confidence to act early and have the conversations that really need to be had.

This book is designed to be useful for many different people. If you are a leader, at any level of your organisation, this book is designed to help you to prevent burnout within your teams. It will give you a greater understanding of what burnout is and why it occurs. It will also provide you with practical skills that will increase your team's ability to help themselves.

I often find that leaders are drawn to work with me because they want to help others, and then realise that they are close to burnout themselves. Therefore, in the last third of the book, I go into some of the specific techniques I have used in my coaching practice when I work 1:1 with clients. These chapters will provide you with ideas for how you can increase something called psychological flexibility, helping you to prevent burnout in yourself and to feel more confident in dealing with whatever life throws at you.

I also hope that the insights and stories will prove valuable to professional coaches who are interested in learning from my experience and the specific coaching approach I use (Acceptance & Commitment Coaching).

The methods I share with you in this book have not just helped my clients, they have had a significant impact on my own life. I am now able to live with my most uncomfortable thoughts and emotions more easily, I feel clearer about what is most important and have a much healthier relationship with myself. I accept my imperfections in a much more compassionate way. Above all, I am so much more confident in my ability to navigate whatever life chooses to throw at me in a skilful way. I want this for you and your colleagues too.

I Am Not Perfect

I want to be upfront with you at the start of our time together. I have more figured out than I did five years ago, and still every day it feels as if there is more to learn. As I sit here and write this book, my mind throws thoughts at me like it's playing a game of darts, trying to find a thought that will hit the bullseye and grab my attention. "Who are you to write this book?" "What a waste of time – nobody will read it," "You should be doing something more productive," "You don't have this stuff fully figured out, so how can you help others?" Aren't our minds interesting. Much more on that later in the book.

I introduce myself as a Business and Coaching Psychologist because I want people to know that I have taken the necessary steps to know what I'm talking about. I am also clear that these titles don't make me more of an expert about you or your unique circumstances than you are. This is one of the reasons why coaching psychology is so appealing to me. It combines the understanding of what it means to be a human, with an approach that puts the individual at the centre of working out their own solutions.

My particular approach to burnout prevention was forged during a painful time in our history. The realities my NHS clients faced as they worked through the Covid pandemic were unprecedented and yet, as you will read in their stories, many of their challenges were the human challenges that so many of us face. They struggled with difficult thoughts, with their relationships with others, with speaking up, with guilt, with grief and with finding ways to put boundaries around their work. Through their stories and my own vulnerability, I want you to know that if life feels like an uphill struggle, you are not alone.

It feels important to say before we go any further that I am not suggesting that the contents of this book replace the importance of going to your GP or therapist if you are struggling. Even though my work is influenced by therapeutic approaches, I am clear that I am not a professional therapist. If you read this book and realise that you are experiencing symptoms of burnout that are having a significant impact on your mental health, please do reach out to your support network (I have also included a list of useful contacts in the Resources section at the back of the book).

The coaching skills I teach in Part Two of this book and in my courses are also not meant to replace your team members getting the professional support they need. The skills I teach are designed as an early intervention tool, supporting you to have everyday conversations that help to prevent burnout over the long-term.

Endings and Beginnings

When we reflect on the significant events of our life, the beginnings that they came from are often clearly visible in retrospect. However, when we are in the middle of an ending, our minds can be so consumed by what we are losing and so uncertain about what's next, that we are blind to the shoots of 'new beginnings' that start poking through.

I often think of burnout as our bodies and minds putting a 'hard stop' on us, forcing an ending of the way we were trying to survive a challenging context that wasn't working for us. It's as if, through this incredibly uncomfortable experience, our mind and body are trying to force us to recognise that something needs to change.

My own unique set of endings and beginnings has led me to write this book. The most significant being my own experience of burnout in 2016, which left me with the overwhelming feeling that I'd failed. At that time, I did not see the green shoots of a path that would lead me to discovering Acceptance & Commitment Therapy (ACT), to support the NHS through the pandemic, then go on to develop a specialism in burnout prevention and start training coaches worldwide in how to use ACT within coaching (also called Acceptance & Commitment Coaching).

I will introduce ACT to you properly in Part Three of the book. ACT's philosophy and tools have not just helped my clients, they have had a significant impact on my own life. Before we get into the skills that helped transform mine and my client's lives, I want to rewind forty-six years and share with you my own story, my own string of endings and beginnings that led me to this book.

Saturday's Child

I was born on a Saturday. I should have known how it would turn out. Do you remember the nursery rhyme about the day of the week you were born? Saturday's Child wasn't fair of face, or full of grace. Oh no, Saturday's Child worked hard for a living. Brilliant.

In my twenties and thirties, I did just that. I pushed myself HARD. I was always working, studying, training for runs and often volunteering on the side. And it worked – I progressed in my career, bought my own flat and collected qualifications like the sew-on badges I'd coveted as a Girl Guide. Deep down I knew I wasn't happy, but I just kept pushing forward, like I was running from something, but I had no idea what it was.

When I became a mother at 37, I was determined to be a role model for independent women, who happened to be mothers, everywhere. I had been offered a significant promotion at work when I was six months pregnant. A role that combined three 'Head of' roles from three different organisations into one. I had never worked at that level before, never managed a team that large and never grown a human before.

As you might have gathered, the way that I deal with fear is to close my eyes and just jump in. I didn't let myself doubt myself for one second. At that time, I felt like I'd finally made it, I was a success! I loved the tight, yet professional, maternity dresses and would stride around in my kitten heels, bump proudly on show, feeling like physical proof that women could have it all.

Motherhood hit me like a freight train. It was like landing on another planet, a planet whose climate I wasn't designed for. My partner and I were one of the first couples to take up the offer of shared parental leave in the UK and I returned to work full time when my daughter was 10 weeks old. I don't have many regrets in my life but if I could turn back time, I'd love to see how things might have been different if I'd made a different choice.

I didn't realise it at the time, but I had postnatal depression. I'm guessing anyone that saw me skipping back into work with a big smile of relief on my face might have guessed that something wasn't quite right. I was just so happy to be back in a place where I felt that I knew the rules. You work ridiculously hard, and you get rewarded.

Looking back, I'm amazed that I made it to eighteen months before experiencing burnout. The immense pressure of the role and the lack of sleep at home was a perfect storm. The strategies that had previously worked in my life, of putting on my 'big girl pants' and just pushing through, were not the strategies that would keep me from burnout's door.

When I reached a crisis point, crying for what seemed like hours in a toilet at work, I felt like such a failure. I had failed at leadership, at motherhood and as a psychologist. I had failed at having it all. I was also embarrassed. My dissertation had been about the psychological benefits of work and here I was, pushed to a place where not only could I not connect to the work I cared about, I couldn't feel anything at all. I was convinced I was broken.

Knowing what I did about my personality, and the way that I approached life's challenges, I took near enough full responsibility for burning out. I believed that there must have been something wrong with me which meant that I hadn't been able to cope with the role. Taking on this responsibility, and making me the problem, although painful, gave me a sense of control over it never happening again.

A New Start

I might not have felt it at the time, but I got lucky. I was offered redundancy from my role, and I decided to do something I'd always wanted to do, start my own business. I trained as a coach and then discovered ACT, which over the next few years, changed my coaching practice and my own life in ways I could never have anticipated.

My business started with a focus on leadership development and business psychology and my passion for helping others quickly evolved into a specialism in resilience. I wanted to help others avoid what I had gone through.

I don't want to leave you with the impression that starting a business is the way to recover from burnout. I quickly discovered that running my own business would test my resilience in different ways to in-house employment. I remember feeling like a fraud when I would stand up and deliver talks on resilience because I knew that it was something that I was still working on for myself. Yes, I got to do work that I enjoyed and a flexibility that enabled me to build an amazing relationship with my daughter after such a rocky start, however the financial insecurity was like a constant little worm in my mind.

At the start I said yes to everything because I was so worried about work suddenly disappearing and I doubted myself at times, which led to some dark days. I also experienced significant anxiety around talking in front of people. I think my fear of public speaking made me keep pushing myself to do it and somehow, I ended up doing work where I felt scared a lot of the time.

The term resilience now turns a lot of people off and I can understand why. People have been told "You're not resilient enough" or "You need to go and get some resilience training." I see now that although I definitely was helping people by supporting them to develop skills to navigate life in a healthy way, by just focusing on the individual, I was ignoring the bigger picture. I was still unconsciously buying into the idea that if I was starting to feel overwhelmed, then I was the problem that needed to be fixed. That if I couldn't cope, it was my fault.

It was going to take an unprecedented, stop-the-world-type event to break this belief in me. Something like a global pandemic might do it.

Maybe it's not All About Me

Please don't judge me, but I used to own a cassette tape of Meatloaf's Bat Out of Hell II album. I remember as a teenager singing, "Life is a lemon and I want my money back." I know, I know, I really was not the cool kid at school. Anyway, I feel like this encapsulates how I was feeling prior to the pandemic. I was still buying into the 'just keep pushing through and if things aren't working, work harder' narrative and even though my body kept giving me warning signs (it felt like I had a cold for ten months of the year) I couldn't see a way out. I was seriously rocking that 'Saturday's Child' energy.

Then the world stopped.

But the world did not stop for everyone. It turned into a living nightmare for many. In March of 2020 I was asked by an NHS Trust to bring together a group of coaches who could provide resilience coaching to staff. I was incredibly grateful for this work, not only because it enabled me to feel as if I was doing something to help but also because I would be able to pay my rent and keep a roof over mine and my daughter's head.

We converted our box room into an office, and I sat there for the next two years delivering coaching session after coaching session. It was a privilege to support these amazing people in a small way. I hope we never forget what they did for us and the sacrifices that so many of them made.

What I was faced with again and again was people who didn't need fixing. They weren't struggling because they weren't resilient enough to cope. They were incredible people working in a terrifying, unpredictable and unrelenting context. Yes, I absolutely could help them to learn skills to navigate this context in the best way possible, but the NHS workers were not the problem – what was being required of them day in and day out both physically and emotionally, was not sustainable.

The Puzzle Pieces Fall into Place

As the peak of the pandemic began to subside, the term 'burnout' became increasingly common. Intrigued, I started to read paper after paper on the topic and the pieces of the puzzle started to fall into place for me. Most of the research points to burnout being a product of our working environment. Yes, there are individual differences, but a common theme is that burnout is an outcome of a context where demands are incredibly high, and resources are low. You could argue that burnout is actually a natural and expected outcome of certain working environments. More on that in Chapter One.

It had been years since I'd experienced burnout, years of me carrying around the belief that if only I'd been better in some way, that I could have coped. The research shouted out a message to me that I needed to hear, a message that I share over and over again:

> If you are feeling burnt out, it's not your fault.

It doesn't mean that we are 'pawns' to our context, there are absolutely things we can do individually and collectively, but burnout does not occur because we are broken in some way – it's not us that needs 'fixing.' What was also clear, the more I read, was that in order for us to avoid burnout, we need to work together to find a way through because we are so much stronger than when we are facing these challenges on our own.

So began my mission to provide coaching and training to support people to help both themselves and others avoid burnout. Without knowing it, I was well on my way down the path which ultimately led me to writing this book.

Structure of the Book

This book looks at burnout prevention in three parts:

- Part 1: Why this book and what is burnout?

- Part 2: How coaching skills can support all of us to prevent burnout in ourselves and others.

- Part 3: How developing psychological flexibility can help us to better navigate life.

This book is written as a both a development tool for yourself and as a tool for you to have more impactful conversations with others. I have intentionally made it practical, because I want you to be able to immediately take the ideas and experiment with integrating them into your life and work. I have included examples from my own life and from my own clients. I have anonymised and fused together different stories to protect the identities of my clients and have gained permission where the details were more likely to identify the individual.

In the first chapter we will explore what burnout is. I hope to demystify the term and increase your understanding of not just what it is, but how it might be prevented.

Part Two mirrors my *Coaching Through Burnout* course. I have tried to write it in a way that has the same feel as the course, by keeping things engaging and experiential. I will be asking you to have a go at applying the tools and ideas for yourself. I really believe that it is through doing the activities that the penny drops for my delegates, so I encourage you to give the activities a go.

In Part Three, I go deeper and share the approach that I use within my coaching psychology practice. I introduce three key ideas from ACT that have been particularly helpful to my clients and in my own life and demonstrate how they can help you to approach life's challenges with greatest confidence and ease.

So, let's start this book at the beginning – what is this thing we call burnout?

1

What is Burnout?

Siobhan and I met in 2022, just after she had been unsuccessful in securing an internal promotion. She had been told that there was no issue with her performance; the reason she hadn't been appointed was because she hadn't answered the questions fully enough. They had not appointed anyone else to the role so suggested she get some interview training and try again in six months. Siobhan was upset and frustrated but pragmatic about the decision. The fact that she had recently turned down an external role she had been offered because she was told that an opportunity was coming up internally had 'rubbed salt into the wounds' a little.

This disappointment occurred for Siobhan in the context of her working eighty-hour weeks due to vacancies and sickness in the team she managed. She shared that she was used to coping in chaotic and pressured environments and had a strong belief in working hard. She often felt penalised for not having children because she felt she couldn't say that she had to get home for them and often ended up being the one working late.

Siobhan's sleep was suffering, she felt exhausted and let down. She knew that the long hours and the amount of work she was doing was having an impact on her health and her relationship at home, but she felt stuck because the work she did and the team she worked with really mattered to her. She felt very deeply that she had to keep pushing through because she didn't want to let people down.

Siobhan was very well thought of by the doctors and staff she supported. She had been instrumental in holding the team together through the pandemic. I met several of her team members whilst doing a wider piece of work and they all shared how much they valued her. They were also deeply concerned because they could see how close to breaking point she was.

What is Burnout?

Burnout crisis point is often the thing that most people associate with burnout. When I say 'I'm burnt out' what I'm saying is that I reached the point where my body and mind said, "ENOUGH!" The point that I could no longer ignore what had been happening to me for months.

The World Health Organisation (WHO) define burnout as "a syndrome conceptualised as resulting from chronic workplace stress that has not been successfully managed" (2019).

Although stress often gets a bad rap, if you play sport or have set yourself goals with deadlines, you know that a little bit of stress can be helpful in focusing our attention on the things we really need to do. Problems start to occur when we experience high levels of stress for a long period of time. When stress goes from an occasional thing to a 'chronic' state, where stress becomes the norm, we are in burnout territory.

This is the thing about burnout, it isn't just about the crisis point, it's about the weeks and months that lead up to that point. In those weeks and months, it is likely that our levels of emotional and physical exhaustion grow significantly, we feel less connected to the things that used to matter to us and the memory of a time when we were able to keep on top of our workload is so distant that the weight of feeling like a failure feels like an old friend.

These three distinct and interconnected symptoms were discovered by social psychologist Christina Maslach and her team in the 1970s and endure today. Let's unpack them.

1. Ineffectiveness and a Lack of Accomplishment

"I feel like I'm letting people down," and "I feel like a failure" are common statements I will hear from people advancing towards a burnout crisis point. Among the many invisible narratives that silently shape our lives there is one that says, "If we are strong/resilient/good enough then we should be able to cope with anything." Our workload increases, our partner loses their job, a colleague leaves and isn't replaced, our parents become ill, our department is restructured, and we feel as if we should be able to just double down and carry on. We are already at full capacity, there is no space to absorb these things that happen.

The demands on us feel so high that we never feel like we get near our to-do list, let alone tick something off it. We try to multitask, we focus on what feels like the most important thing, the crisis right in front of us. We 'firefight' never getting to the longer-term initiatives that could help us to work more effectively. We are told we aren't strategic enough and in the same breath are asked if we can take on the management of another team whose manager left and can't be replaced because there is a hiring freeze. We see our teams start to strain and, fearing that they might burnout, we take more on ourselves.

Leadership researcher Nick Petrie has conducted extensive research on burnout and states that, "We didn't meet many selfish people who burned out. Instead, it was the most committed, most collaborative and hard-working people who sacrificed themselves. In other words, your best people," (2023). I absolutely agree with this and see it in my clients every day.

When we are so used to coping and to pushing through, it is no wonder that the mechanism for deciding when we have extended ourselves beyond what is humanly possible is our health. The amount we care may be infinite but the amount of emotional and physical energy we are able to give and stay OK is finite.

2. Overwhelming Exhaustion

When we are exhausted, it can feel like we have been giving and giving and we just don't have anything left to give. We reach a point where we think, "If one more person asks me for five minutes, I'm going to lose my s***." Although Christina Maslach's initial research focused on emotional exhaustion, this was expanded to include exhaustion more generally, encompassing physical and cognitive exhaustion, as more research was conducted. It feels as if modern life requires us to be there emotionally for others, to make increasing complex decisions and to keep pushing our bodies through, even when we desperately need a rest. When this is all happening at once, then the sense of exhaustion becomes compounded.

Sleep is one of the first things that stress impacts. We work late and then struggle to switch off and/or are woken by our minds in the middle of the night reminding us of the things we need to do in the morning. I used to be guilty of getting up and just doing the work in the middle of the night because that felt better than lying there worrying, unable to get back to sleep.

I'm sure that I don't need to list the research on the benefits of sleep to convince you how important it is for things like decision-making, motivation and mood. Life just feels harder when we're tired. What's also interesting about sleep is the important part it plays in supporting us to process our emotions. If we aren't getting enough sleep, then this will impact our ability to deal with the emotional demands of our work (and life). If you are struggling with sleep, in the resources section I've included a link to some great advice from the charity Mind that you might find helpful.

Emotional demands become an issue when they hang around with nowhere to go. Most of us were not taught how to process emotions. When we experience an uncomfortable emotion that we don't like, or absorb a difficult emotion from a colleague/client/family member, we push it down or pop it in our 'emotional backpack,' so we can quickly move on to the next thing we need to do.

Often, we use distraction tactics to avoid feeling things in the moment. My phone is my go-to emotional avoidance device, but for others it can be sweet treats, TV, alcohol, shopping etc. There is absolutely nothing wrong with these things (I enjoy them all!) and in the moment they might feel like the most helpful thing to do or consume. However, if we are doing them consistently in service of emotional avoidance, over time that backpack is going to get heavier and heavier, and our health (and wallet) will suffer too.

We might even get to the point where it feels as if there is no room left to fit anything else in, but the emotions keep coming. Then something small happens, the strap breaks and all the emotions we have been packing away flood out across the floor.

Not only are we not taught how to process our emotions, for many of us, we grew up in homes where emotions were to be avoided at all costs. When I finally went to get help from a therapist, I discovered that I found it incredibly difficult even to name the emotion I was experiencing. I will talk more about emotions in Part Three but if you recognise any of this in yourself, I recommend the investment in talking therapy.

The topic of burnout is littered with vicious cycles, where the strategies we use to try and cope with the demands we are facing result in us inadvertently speeding up our advance towards crisis point. In the case of emotions, the 'backpack strategy' increases the chance of us reaching emotional overwhelm, which itself brings up uncomfortable emotions, which we then pop into our overflowing backpack.

The same goes for recovery. It can feel like the best thing to do to recover is to lie on the sofa and watch something mindless on the TV or your phone. In fact, it can feel like the only thing we have the energy to do. However, it's important to understand how we best recover. If we've been sitting all day and then sit down again as our way of recovery, we can feel even more sluggish. Active forms of recovery like going for a walk, or taking part in a hobby we enjoy, can be a much better way for us to recover (even though instinctively we want to lie down). When it comes to sleep, we know that physical activity in the day, especially if it involves getting outside in the morning, supports us to get a good night's sleep. So again, we are in a place where the thing we instinctively want to do doesn't help us in the long run.

3. Cynicism and Detachment

When something is causing us pain, it makes sense that we start to distance ourselves from it. I hear clients saying, "It's not just that I don't care anymore, it's that I can't care anymore." They recognise that caring deeply about their work, and the conscientiousness and hard work that comes from caring so much, has hurt them. They want my help with caring less, believing that if they cared less, they would be more able to put their own needs first.

In the workplace, caring less can outwardly look like someone who is disengaged in team meetings, who feels that the organisation doesn't care about them or says things like "Wouldn't this job be great without any patients/customers/colleagues!". Humour at work can help us to maintain perspective, and laughter can help us to connect to others and process emotions in difficult situations. The thing to notice is when this tips over into resignation and cynicism, and the hope feels as if it has been sucked out.

When we feel as if we are unable to control what happens to us, we can develop a sense of something psychologist Martin Seligman called 'learned helplessness' (1972), where we don't even try to change our situation because we are so used to nothing improving that we give up trying.

The more I worked with clients experiencing cynicism and detachment, the more that I noticed that often there was a values challenge at the route of their disengagement. We will explore values in Chapter 11 where I will share that when we care deeply about something (Service, Compassion, Equality, Fairness, Quality, etc.) and it gets ignored or denied, or, because of resource limitations, we don't have the opportunity to fully express that value, then it absolutely makes sense that we start to distance and protect ourselves.

Why is Burnout Predominantly a Workplace Issue?

Much of the research on burnout has been focused on the workplace. The WHO definition, explicitly describing burnout as a 'workplace phenomenon' reflects this research and I suspect also has the intention of highlighting the responsibility of organisations to take burnout seriously. It also reinforces the need to not make burnout about the individual, but about the context they are working in.

Every day my clients give me examples of demands they are facing from both their work AND their home life. I also see how conflict between these different domains can contribute to the symptoms of burnout (flashback to home schooling and ordering a bottle of Pimms in an 'essentials' box from Amazon during the pandemic).

Why Do We Burnout?

This leads us nicely to the working conditions that can result in burnout. The 'Job Demand-Resources' model of burnout (Bakker & Demerouti, 2007), provides a really helpful starting point to have conversations about what is within our collective control to change about our working environments, in order to reduce the risk of burnout.

The model states that when demands on us are high and the resources we have access to are low, we are more likely to experience exhaustion (from the high demands) and disengagement (from low resources), and therefore are at greater risk of burning out.

What Demands are You Facing?

When workloads are high, when you are under tight time pressures, if your physical or psychological environment is unsafe, if your work shifts and you face complexity in relationships, the Job Demands-Resources model states that you are more likely to experience exhaustion.

In many ways, this feels like a no-brainer. They are the things that many of us face. What feels important is that the research tells us that these are the things that can contribute to exhaustion, chronic stress and burnout. When the WHO is saying that burnout is about 'chronic workplace stress that has not been managed' it is saying that organisations have a responsibility to keep an eye on these things and take action if they are having a detrimental impact.

What Resources are Available to You?

If you are not receiving feedback, if your rewards don't seem fair, if you lack control over how, when and where you do your job, if you aren't able to participate in decision-making, or if you have low job security and lack supervisor support, you are more likely to report being disengaged in your work.

On the flipside, when organisations recognise their employees are facing high demands and put energy and investment into increasing the resources that their employees have access to, they can reduce the chance of staff becoming disengaged and burning out.

Resources can also be internal too, and this is where something called psychological flexibility can be particularly helpful. In Part Three of this book, I will be sharing ideas which have helped my clients (and myself) to build psychological flexibility and inner resources.

Organisational Risk Factors

Maslach & Leiter (2016) shared two decades of research on burnout which identified six clear risk factors for burnout across many occupations in various countries: Workload, control, reward, community, fairness, values. Their message was similar to Bakker and Demerouti: If our workloads are high, if we have limited autonomy, if we don't feel fairly rewarded or treated, if we feel isolated or our personal values are challenged by our organisation's actions, then we are more likely to experience burnout.

Alternatively, if our workload feels manageable, we have some control over decision-making, feel fairly rewarded and treated, in an organisation with a strong sense of community that aligns with our values, then we are less likely to experience burnout.

How Can We Prevent Burnout?

The more I read about burnout, and work with people experiencing symptoms of burnout, the more I believe that we can't do it alone. Yes, there are things we can do ourselves AND we also must address the contexts we are working in. It feels like this is the leadership challenge of our age, particularly in industries under massive demand pressure, like the NHS.

In order to reduce the demands we collectively face, and increase our resources, we have to approach it from all levels, looking at roles, teams, organisations and systems. In my work with teams, I facilitate conversations about what is within the team's control in relation to reducing demands and increasing resources. I believe strongly that this should be a topic that is regularly on every leadership team's meeting agenda.

I see these conversations happening when burnout has already taken a strong hold on a team and people are collectively feeling close to breaking point. This is a difficult place to come back from without an injection of financial resource or tough decisions about what activities will need to be stopped. Let's learn from the teams that have reached this point and act as soon as we start to see the cracks of exhaustion, disengagement and a sense of ineffectiveness appearing.

As well as these collective interventions to make our working environments ones where we can both do good work and stay well, there is also a place for helping individuals to increase their confidence in dealing with challenging environments. People's experience of burnout is different, and our perception of demands and resources will also be different. This is one of the reasons I believe that people are attracted to coaching. In a coaching intervention you won't get a 'sheep dip' approach to avoiding burnout, you will have the opportunity to work out a way forward that works for you. You work on solutions that work for your mind, body and context.

Above all, to prevent burnout, I believe that we must make and protect space to have good conversations. We also need to feel confident that we have the skills that enable us to have conversations that truly make a difference.

That is the core aim of this book. To help you, in the limited time you have available, to have the best burnout preventing conversations possible.

PART 2

How Conversations Can Help Prevent Burnout

2

The Power of Conversation

We met Siobhan at the beginning of the last chapter. The goal Siobhan had for coaching was simple, she wanted to come into work, do one job and go home. She felt that she was being asked to do extra things with little consideration of what she already had on her plate. Siobhan acknowledged that she had reached a point where she felt she needed to be clear with her manager that things could not carry on the way they were because she was going to break. The current situation was not sustainable for her or the department. There was also no motivation for others to do anything differently because everything was still getting done.

In our coaching space we focused our attention on how 'workable' Siobhan's current situation was and on the small changes that were in her control. We started with finding ways for her to get the headspace to step back and see what actions she could take. She decided to start with boundary setting. Siobhan focused on finding places to work uninterrupted, on booking in leave, and on being clearer with her manager about her current workload and the work she was not able to get to within her core working hours.

She also worked on how she responded to requests for her to do additional work, saying things like, "I could do it, however it will mean I can't do..." to make people aware of the impact of new requests. She discovered that when she challenged back, nothing terrible happened; and saying 'no' didn't mean she was a bad person, she just had other important things to do.

At the end of four coaching sessions, Siobhan wasn't doing as much extra work. She had set much clearer boundaries around the work she did and didn't do. She had also lowered her expectations of what she should be doing, so when she had lots of emails, she didn't try and respond to them all; she knew that people would call if it was urgent.

Siobhan shared that coaching gave her the space to think about what she wanted and what she needed to do. She had reconnected with how respected and cared for the doctors she supported made her feel, which linked to her values. She had a holiday booked in the diary and felt happier in her job. Things weren't perfect but she was in a place where she felt able to make changes that had a chance of leading to lasting, sustainable improvements. Importantly, she also encouraged more conversations in her wider team about what was possible and sustainable in relation to workload.

I reached out to Siobhan as I was writing this book because I wanted to share her powerful story as it was and knew that, even with a change of name, she might be able to identify herself. Not only was Siobhan happy for her story to be shared, but she was also keen that I share an update of where she is two years later:

> "I must say, without the help of your coaching, I wouldn't be where I am today. I do minimal out of hours work and have taken up a social hobby that gives me great distraction from the day-to-day work dilemmas. It gives me a reason to book frequent time off and since my openness with peers, there is a better environment in the office. It was mentioned in my recent 1-2-1 with my line manager how they can see a difference in my character being brighter than previously."

Could Coaching Conversations Help More People Like Siobhan?

Where do you tend to have your flashes of inspiration? Ideas often come to me in the shower. Most of them get forgotten, they run down the drain like the bubbles from my shampoo. Some hang on in there though, and quietly, yet persistently whisper in my ear. The connection between burnout prevention and coaching skills was one of those ideas.

I had been delivering coaching to NHS staff like Siobhan, and clients from a range of different professions, all through the Covid pandemic. For many, the initial focus had been on staying resilient. As time went on and we entered the second and third year, there was a noticeable increase in levels of exhaustion, and burnout started to be a term that was more widely used. I could see how helpful coaching was to my clients in relation to staying both mentally and physically well. I also supported many of them to take more of a coaching approach with their teams, helping them to manage their workloads and build capability.

When I had the opportunity to bid for a piece of work to support burnout prevention from my local NHS Integrated Care Board, I decided to take a punt and proposed delivering two *Coaching Through Burnout* courses. These courses would teach delegates about burnout and would also give them some foundational coaching skills. The aim was to increase their confidence in having good quality conversations, which could support the prevention of burnout in themselves and others.

When the courses were advertised, I was overwhelmed by the number of people who wanted to attend. Both courses were full within a day and within a week I had a waiting list with hundreds of names on it. Luckily, over the next eighteen months the wonderful commissioner of the course was able to beg, steal and borrow the money to run more courses and I ended up training more than 150 leaders from across the NHS system in Hampshire.

The feedback that I received from this course was incredible. The topic and the content just seemed to resonate with where people were at. The pandemic had left people incredibly tired. They had rallied together in a time of crisis and needed to rest and recover but there was no time for this. There had also been no time to process the emotional impact of the terrible things they had lived and worked through. Knowing more about what burnout is, helped them to make sense of what they were feeling. The course also gave them practical skills that they could apply immediately to improve things for themselves and their colleagues. One of the delegates wrote:

> "This course is one of the few I could ever say was entirely worthwhile and will have substantial and long-lasting impact both on my practice going forward with my team, the colleagues I work with outside of my team and also on my own behaviour and levels of burnout."

Receiving so many positive pieces of feedback like this was an emotional experience. I felt as if I was making a difference to a group of people who really needed support. It inspired me to take the teaching from the *Coaching Through Burnout* course and share it with even more people. That is what Part Two is all about.

The Focus of Part Two

In the next five chapters I have attempted to take the key coaching skills elements of the *Coaching Through Burnout* course and deliver them to you in 'book form.'

I deliberately made the course highly experiential, with very few slides, because I believe that when it comes to coaching skills, we can understand them intellectually, but to actually change our habitual, and often unconscious behaviour, we need to practise doing the things we've learnt many times.

When I initially started writing these chapters, they quickly became long and heavy. I'm sitting here now with the print outs of the original chapters next to me. Even though it's taken hours to write them I'm going to be bold and strip it back in a way that more closely represents the course I deliver.

This means that for the next five chapters you will be asked lots of reflective questions, I will highlight key messages and I will be encouraging you to experiment with the activities I share. I have to be honest, when I read books that ask me to go and do things, I have a tendency to want to keep reading and think I'll come back to the activity later (yet rarely do). If you are like me, I want to encourage you to stop and give the activity a go. I have no doubt you will get a lot from the chapters by just reading them, but you'll get even more by giving the activities a try.

What is a Coaching Conversation?

When I teach coaching skills, I am not teaching the delegates to be professional coaches who deliver coaching in the typical hour-long dedicated sessions. I am teaching people how to take the skills that coaches use within a coaching session and embed them into their everyday interactions.

So, what is a 'Coaching Conversation'? If you were eavesdropping on a coaching conversation, what would you expect to observe? You might observe some of these things:

- One person is doing a lot more listening and a lot less talking than the other person. In a standard conversation we might expect it to be about 50/50 in the balance of talking to listening. For a coaching conversation, if we were the one taking a coaching approach, we would be listening for 80% or even 90% of the time.

- When the person taking the coaching approach does speak, we would expect to hear them asking questions and maybe also summarising and clarifying what they have heard.

- If we read their body language and listened to the way they were speaking, we would notice that they were being empathetic, supportive, and non-judgemental and we might notice that the person doing most of the talking looks like a person who feels safe in sharing their challenges.

- If we listened closely to the questions being asked, we might get the sense that the person asking them believed that the other person had the ability to change and to come up with their own ideas for ways to move forward.

Coaching skills can help us to be truly useful to each other because when someone holds a coaching space for you, they help you to think better for yourself. They support you to develop your own problem-solving skills. They give you their attention in a way that makes you feel safe and that you matter.

How Can Coaching Conversations Help to Prevent Burnout?

When we are focused on using our conversations to help to prevent burnout, coaching skills can be helpful both for the person taking a coaching approach and for the person they are using a coaching approach with.

As a reminder, the three 'symptoms' of burnout are: overwhelming exhaustion, cynicism and detachment and feeling ineffective. Let's look at the benefits of a coaching approach from those three perspectives:

Overwhelming Exhaustion

A coaching conversation can be a space to just pause for a moment. To step off the 'hamster wheel' and just look around and within ourselves. It can also be a space which can support us to get some things off our chest, enabling us to process some of the emotions we've been trying to control. Being asked coaching questions can help us to take a step out of the challenges we are facing and see them with new eyes. It's a space where we can be supported to reflect on boundaries and to work out an approach to the actions we need to take, and the conversations that need to be had. We can be supported to work out what we want to be different and what is really important to us.

Cynicism and Detachment

Just the act of being listened to helps us to feel cared for and not alone in our challenges. A coaching conversation can help us to recognise how our environment might be contributing to feelings of being burnt out, and what might be within our control to change. As we start to control the things within our control, we might feel more able to have wider conversations with our colleagues and our manager about what we feel needs to change for work to feel more sustainable. When we are asked questions about what is working in our lives and about the things that bring us joy and meaning to us, it can help us to reconnect to the positive in our lives and to see our challenges from different perspectives.

Feeling Ineffective

When we are feeling ineffective, we might feel overwhelmed by everything we need to do. Coaching conversations can help us to build our capacity and capability to solve our own problems. We can be supported to prioritise and work out what is within our control. We can notice how behaviours, like trying to do everything ourselves, can be speeding up our advance towards a burnout 'crisis point.' As we are supported to come up with our own solutions and start to implement them, our self-confidence and self-efficacy (feeling as if we can create change) can increase.

There are also benefits for you, the person taking a coaching approach. You feel as if you helped someone to help themselves. If you are a line manager, taking a coaching approach with your team can result in you taking on less work yourself to protect your team. You are also building capability, capacity and confidence in your team, meaning that they are less likely to be asking you for help in the future.

What Gets in the Way of Having Coaching Conversations?

Reflect for a moment on your day and the types of conversations you have. What might get in the way of you taking a coaching approach to conversations?

You might have felt that there was a skills element, which I hope these chapters will help you with. You may have struggled to even think about the style of conversations you have because so much of it is unconscious. I hope chapter four will help you with this. You may also have thought the thing that many of my delegates tell me, "The reason I don't listen and ask questions more is because I don't have **time**."

When time is limited, and our life is incredibly busy, it feels quicker and easier to give someone a solution or to be directive than it is to take more of a coaching approach. If you feel this way, I hear you. It is a logical thing to think, particularly when our mind is in short-term survival mode. What I hope to prove to you in the coming chapters is that it doesn't need to take as much time as you might think **and** the time it does take is an investment into much bigger longer-term gains.

I passionately believe that:

*When time is limited, the quality of your conversations matters even more **and** when so many things feel out of your control, something that **is** within your control is the quality of your conversations.*

Learning coaching skills isn't difficult, the challenge is that it involves a change to our very well practised and unconscious current conversational styles. To change behaviour, we have to bring our current unconscious behaviour into conscious awareness. That's the focus for the next two chapters.

Let's get started.

3

Do I Have Your Full Attention?

When someone gives you their full attention, what are they saying to you? When I ask this question in the workshops I deliver, I usually get answers like this: "It says that they care," or "They are telling me they are interested," or "They are saying that I'm important."

When you give someone your full attention, what you are saying, without needing to say anything is *"In this moment, you are the most important thing to me."* Just sit with that for a moment. There are so many things that feel out of our control in this world and yet we have within our power something that can show another person that they matter. It's the reason why I often say: *"The greatest gift you can give someone is your attention."*

The Battle for Our Attention

I finished a coaching call yesterday, picked my phone off the desk, and headed downstairs. I started to rotate through the usual Apps as I walked into the kitchen. Glancing at my partner, I asked him how his day was and then 'listened' to his response whilst responding to a WhatsApp message.

I really hope that I am not the only one who shows up better in their work than they do at home. What's particularly frustrating is that I know how powerful giving someone your full attention is. It is a really important part of my coaching approach. When you work with me, you get as close to my full attention as is humanly possible. I recognise that this might be the only place where my client gets this quality of attention. It matters.

And yet, when I'm with the people I love most in the world, I signal to them that responding to a message or checking in on Instagram is more important than they are. What is that about? Being present with the people I love is one of the things I need to practise the most; and if I'm honest, I haven't cracked it. I'm a work in progress.

It's not that any of us walk around intentionally denying people the opportunity to know that we care, we are constantly bombarded by people and technology looking to grab our attention. The more we get used to working in a distracted way, the more it becomes normal and the more our mind learns to expect the distraction. This means that we are also not training our minds how to fully attend to something in the face of distractions.

It's important to say that our brains are all different, so full attention looks different for different people. The challenges around full attention are also different depending on the brain we have. This is not my area of expertise, so I have recommended books in the 'Further Reading' section if you want to know more about neurodiversity.

What are Your Biggest Distractors?

Think for a moment about a normal day. What are the things that get in the way of you giving other people (or activities you are engaged in) your full attention?

In a world where so many things feel out of our control, recognising our biggest distractors and taking action to limit their impact on us is one thing that is within our control. A couple of years ago, I was driving and saw on my Apple watch that I had an email from a tricky client. I didn't read it, but I spent the whole of the rest of the drive worrying about what the email was about.

It suddenly occurred to me that having emails appear on my watch was a default setting that I had just accepted. At that moment I woke up to the fact that it wasn't healthy for my emails to be able to hijack my attention and that it was absolutely my choice about what notifications I received.

Maybe this resonates with you. What 'default settings' are hijacking your attention? Maybe it's Teams notifications when you're doing work that requires full concentration or WhatsApp group messages that would be better on 'mute.' Why not take a moment now to do a quick audit of your technology settings and reset them as needed.

The Myth of Multitasking

One of the areas where it feels we are continuing to train ourselves to work in a distracted way is online meetings. There is absolutely no judgement here because I find it incredibly hard to just focus on what is happening on the screen if I'm a participant of a training session. My mind is convinced I can multitask. I keep one ear on what's happening on the screen and then I'll sneakily answer an email or scan through social media on my phone.

We think we can multitask, but study after study (e.g. Madore & Wagner, 2019) has shown that we can only attend to one sensory input at a time. If we're really honest, for those of us who look at our phones and think they can watch TV at the same time, we will have had times where we had to rewind the TV because we missed something important to the plot while looking at our phone. You also might own up to being caught out on an online meeting when someone says your name and you have absolutely no idea what they asked you because you were doing something else (I always find a hasty, "Sorry, you froze for a moment there, can you repeat that?" works a treat in that situation!).

When we try to split our attention, the skill we are training ourselves to do is to switch attention quickly between different tasks and different sensory inputs. The problem with this is not only do we then struggle when we need to just attend to one thing (like when we are listening to another person), it is also incredibly cognitively fatiguing to be constantly switching from one thing to another. Not what we want when we are trying to avoid exhaustion.

Our Environments Often Don't Help

On NHS wards there are alarms and buzzers and many conversations going on all at once. Even if someone is lucky enough to have an office, there are often colleagues popping in to ask questions (even with a 'Do Not Disturb' sign on the door). I've had people share with me that they have ended up having meetings in cupboards just so they can have a quiet, confidential and uninterrupted conversation! Choosing where we have a meeting can have a huge impact on our ability to give someone our full attention. Think about the conditions that help you to concentrate and listen well. What environments naturally have less distractions for you?

Walking can be a really great way to both have a good conversation and get some fresh air and exercise. Although making eye contact is often seen as an important part of good listening, you may have noticed that conversations that happen when we are side by side with each other, not making eye contact, can enable us to be more vulnerable. I definitely notice that I will save trickier conversations with my partner for a long walk or car drive (maybe that's partly because he is unable to escape).

Instead of having onscreen catch-ups with colleagues, I'll often ask if we can go 'old school' and talk to each other on the phone while we both go out for a quick walk. Sometimes just experimenting with different ways to communicate without distractions can help us to improve our conversations.

Have You Got Five Minutes?

When I've taught these skills in the NHS, the conversation has often come around to what to do when someone asks you if you have five minutes, and you really want to help them, but you really don't have five minutes. We explore how being open with them can be much more supportive than getting yourself into a situation where you are likely to end up being distracted and not giving them the best quality interaction. It's OK to be honest. You could even see it as an opportunity to role model showing someone that you care without sacrificing your own needs.

Instead of saying yes and then having an internal narrative going off about what you feel you should be doing, you could instead say: "I am just about to leave to go to a meeting" or "I'm in the middle of writing a report" or "I'm dealing with an urgent issue… and I know that I won't be able to give you the full attention that you deserve right now. Is it something that can wait until tomorrow or is there anyone else who might be able to help you?" Sharing with others that we want to give them full attention and that we can't in that moment can be incredibly powerful.

It's Not Just Our External Environment that Can Distract Us

It's important to say here that in order to give someone our full attention, we not only have to deal with the distractions going on around us, but we also have our own thoughts trying to grab our attention. Our mind likes to remind us of the things we need to do, comment on an email we received earlier, make judgments about things we can see around us. It is so easy to 'hook' onto one of those thoughts and follow it down a rabbit hole. In Chapters 10 and 12, I will share some ideas for how we can navigate these internal distractions.

Improving Our Listening

Once we have the conditions right for giving someone our full attention, we can then focus on listening well. A standard conversation can feel a little like a tennis match, we each take it in turns to speak, batting the topics back and forth between us. This means that while the other person is speaking, we are focusing less on what they are saying and more on how and when we are going to respond.

As Steven Covey famously said in his book *The Seven Habits of Highly Effective People* (1989), "we are often listening to respond rather than to understand." When we listen to respond, our attention is taken up by waiting for the pause where we can jump in. Our mind is busy thinking of examples, advice or questions we can ask. We are making all the signs that we are listening, but the truth is that we are jumping forward and back from listening and preparing to respond.

When we are listening to understand, we step out of standard conversational convention. We let go (as much as we are able) of what we are going to do next. We take in what we are being told, we tune in to the other person's body language, we connect to the emotions they are displaying. When they pause, we leave a space for them to say more.

Listen then Pause

It is interesting that one of the conversational fears we have is silence. Many delegates on my courses have shared that they don't want to look stupid if they don't have anything prepared to say. It is a skill in itself to get comfortable with silence. What's interesting is that once we start to leave pauses, the other person often starts talking again. I've also observed that the length of perceived silence is much longer for the person who feels they should speak next than it is for the person who has been speaking.

I'm hoping that this chapter has got you thinking about how you might improve the attention you give and the listening you do. The absolute best way to do this is by setting an experiment for yourself. I invite you to do something that I ask the delegates that attend my courses to do, the 'And what else' listening exercise.

The 'And what else?' Listening Experiment

This exercise is inspired by the work of Nancy Klein (1999). It's an activity you can practise while in conversation with a friend, during a work supervision or maybe with a partner/flatmate when you get home from work.

1. Ask someone a nice open question, something like, "What have you got coming up that you are most excited about?" or "What went well today/this week/this month?" or "What would you say is your biggest challenge at the moment?"

2. Once you have asked the question, I want you to consciously notice what your mind instinctively wants you to do. Notice when thoughts start to pull you away and consciously bring your attention back to listening.

3. When the other person takes a breath, just let the pause sit there for a bit and see if they say anything else.

4. If it feels like they need you to say something, invite them to say more in a very open way. You might say something like, "That's interesting; tell me more about that," or "And what else?"

5. Aim to do this for at least five minutes.

When you've finished, take a moment to reflect on the following things.

A. What did your mind want you to do?
You might have been able to stick to my 'rules' and you might not have. There is no judgement here – many of my delegates find this exercise incredibly challenging because it involves stopping doing a range of things that we've been unconsciously doing for years. What's more important is noticing what your mind wants you to do. Maybe it was to ask a question, say something encouraging,

offer some advice or share your own experience. Jot these things down. They will be useful data for later chapters. Right now, I want you to mull over this point.

*If you had asked a question at any point, you would have taken the conversation in the direction of **your interest** and away from where the other person's mind was taking them.*

When we do anything other than listen, we are influencing the direction of the conversation.

B. What would you like to put back into your conversations?

In the experiment we stripped out all our natural human conversational behaviour. It probably felt a bit clunky and unnatural because I asked you to take so much of what you would normally do out. It's now time to think about what you might want to put back in. This will be different for each of us, but generally the conversational elements that you might want to put back in are:

- Empathy: Saying things like, "That sounds really tough" or "I can see how upset that has made you."
- Words of encouragement and support: Things like "That sounds brilliant" or "You should be really proud of yourself."
- Repeating or summarising to show you have listened and to check your understanding.

C. What will you do differently?

In the final part of our reflection, I want you to think about the impact that this experiment had on you. Some of the things I hear from my delegates are:

- "I can't believe how much I learnt about this person in five minutes."
- "It made me realise how often I jump in with advice – I had to physically sit on my hands to stop myself."
- "It was actually quite nice to relax and just listen."

Was there anything specific that you noticed?

If you feel able to, you could ask the other person how the conversation felt for them. When I run this listening experiment with groups, some of the things I hear from the person being listened to are:

- "I relaxed when I realised I wasn't going to be interrupted."
- "I felt like the other person was empathising, even though they weren't saying anything."
- "I felt really safe to share my story."

The listener frequently will report that it felt strange to be listened to for so long, which I think tells us a lot about how rarely we receive good quality listening.

Hopefully I've given you some things to think about in relation to how you can increase the quality of the attention you give. You've now got a great foundation to have even better conversations. Now let's explore how our attempts to be helpful can sometimes have unintended consequences…

4

Conversation Traps

Take a moment to reflect on a time when you've shared with someone that you were struggling, and you received a well-meaning but not-so-helpful response. What did they say to you? Some people jump in with advice, trying to be helpful. Others share their own challenges to let us know we are not alone. You might have experienced being dismissed with a, "It'll be fine" or received an attempt to cheer you up with an "At least you've got…" Some people will want to fix it for you and will try and take your challenges off your plate.

These are all very human and very understandable ways of responding, coming from a place of really wanting to help. Unfortunately, they can have unintended consequences. I want you to take a moment and reflect about how it felt to be on the receiving end of the response you got. How did you leave that conversation feeling?

When we discuss these types of responses in the workshops I deliver, the participants share that, even though they recognise that the person had good intentions, the response they get to sharing that they are struggling has often left them feeling that they haven't really been heard or that what they are feeling isn't valid.

What is clear seems too obvious to say, but I will say it anyway. When we share with someone that we are struggling, the most important thing that we need is just for someone to hear us. Really hear us. Not listening whilst thinking of a response, or working out what advice to give us, or waiting for us to take a breath so they can talk about themselves. Listening with the sole intention of understanding what we are saying to them.

What this means is that to be more useful to people who are at risk of burnout, we have some 'unlearning' to do.

Conversation Traps

What we need to 'unlearn' are all the conversational habits or 'traps' we have picked up over the years. I'm not suggesting that these conversational habits need to be hunted down and eradicated from our behaviour (if that were even possible). However, when our intention is to support someone else to work through a challenge, falling into these not-so-helpful ways of responding, although well intentioned, can result in a missed opportunity for a good quality, useful conversation.

In my work, I have identified five common traps, which I have turned into five personas. As you read through these five personas, I invite you to reflect on your go-to ways of responding. There is no judgement here. These ways of responding are well intentioned, very human and all have their place in our conversational repertoire. It's when they become habitual and not in service of what the other person really needs, that a tweak in our response might be needed. Let's meet these five personas.

The Advice-Giver

What is Their Intention?
The advice-giver really wants to help. As soon as you have started to share your problem with them, their mind is already working on solutions that they will be itching to share with you. They can be like a child in a classroom wriggling while sitting on their hands, desperate to say, "I know this one!"

They are so proud of their ability to problem solve that when someone comes to them with problems, they feel useful when they can give them a solution. It may even be that their feeling of self-worth has become linked to their ability to solve other people's problems.

What Might They Say?
The advice giver's response might sound something like, "Have you thought about…?" or "What I think you need to do is…"

What Might the Unintended Consequence Be?
Advice from others can feel welcome when you feel stuck. However, it may be a solution that would work for them but not for you. You can be left feeling like the other person is better than you because they know more and could come up with a simple solution that you hadn't thought of. This can knock your confidence.

Also, you haven't been the one to solve your problem, so you've missed out on the opportunity to think it through and build your confidence in your ability to solve problems like this in the future.

For someone experiencing signs of burnout, the exhausted part of them might welcome someone else telling them what to do but it can also feed into their sense of being ineffective. If it's a solution that isn't a good fit for them, it could also end up feeling like another thing to add to their to-do list that they don't really want to do, or feel they have the time to do.

When Might this Strategy Be Appropriate?

Giving advice absolutely has its place. If we have a new member of staff who is unlikely to be able to know what might be possible, or if we are in a high-risk situation, where it is safer to tell someone what you think they should do, advice giving is appropriate.

The risk of using the advice-giving strategy all the time is that we will miss opportunities to help other people to think through their own problems and build their problem-solving capability.

The Rescuer

What is Their Intention?

So many of us love to 'fix' and to make life better for others. Whilst the 'Advice-giver' leaves us to go and action the solution they have given us, the 'Rescuer' takes it further. They take it upon themselves to fix the issue for us. Before we have even finished telling them what's wrong, they are already messaging someone who can help or have cleared their diary in their head so they can do the task that needs doing.

What Might They Say?
Advice givers might respond with a "Please don't worry. I'll sort it," or "I know the exact person who can help, I'll message them now."

What Might the Unintended Consequence Be?
Although in the short term it might feel good to be rescued, over time there is a risk that it can dent our confidence and leave us feeling as if we can't really cope. When someone rescues us, we lose an opportunity to problem-solve for ourselves. We can get into a position where, whenever we are struggling, we always go to the 'Rescuer' rather than trying to work it through ourselves.

For someone experiencing the symptoms of burnout, if they are in overwhelm, being 'rescued' might be exactly what they need. However, if rescuing becomes the go-to response they receive when they share that they are struggling, it risks decreasing their self-confidence and their sense of self-efficacy (their belief that they have the ability to create change in their life). When we feel this way, we feel a lack of control which can feed into feelings of ineffectiveness, and we can become detached from feeling connected to our role, as we struggle with the emotions of worrying that we might not be good enough.

When we look through the lens of burnout prevention, there is also a potential impact on the 'Rescuer'. If they have a habit of taking on additional work to protect others, they are probably also reluctant to delegate to someone who they perceive might be struggling. This increase in their own workload in turn increases the demands that they are facing and could lead to them experiencing the signs of burnout themselves.

When Might this Strategy Be Appropriate?

When someone is feeling overwhelmed, stressed or emotional they may need you to just listen to them, or they might benefit from a walk around the block or the British solution for everything – a cup of tea. If their stress levels are high, they will probably find it very hard, in that moment, to properly think things through for themselves. This is the kind of moment that it feels right to sit down together, go through their challenges, and take away any that would alleviate their immediate suffering. To balance out the 'rescuing', you could also suggest that you meet up again later to chat through some longer-term solutions (that they can take the lead on).

The Happy-Maker

What is Their Intention?

Several few months ago, I phoned up Mum to tell her that my house sale had fallen through. Her response was, "Well, at least you have the weekend to look forward to!" Great. Another insight into why I became a psychologist (love you Mum!). The 'Happy-Maker' wants to point out something that they believe will distract us from our pain and make us feel good again. It may be because they feel a deep responsibility to make the people around them happy, or maybe they feel uncomfortable with difficult emotions. There are many reasons that people might 'happy-make,' it might even be a habitual response they learnt in childhood. I know I have to catch myself trying to cheer my daughter up with a sugary treat when she is upset (maybe 'happy-making' is hereditary…).

What Might They Say?
The 'Happy-Maker' loves the words 'at least' – "At least you've got…." or "At least it wasn't something worse." Or they might try something more philosophical like: "I'm sure you'll look back on this and realise that it was a blessing in disguise."

What Might the Unintended Consequences Be?
I got off that phone call with my Mum pretty damn quickly and called someone that I knew would give me what I needed at that moment. Although I knew that my Mum wasn't intentionally trying to upset me, I was left with the sense that maybe how I was feeling wasn't OK and that I should just get over it and move on. I had feelings that I just needed to get out so I could process them. Even though she didn't mean it, I was left feeling disconnected, like she didn't really understand where I was emotionally.

When Might this Strategy Be Appropriate?
I think this one is about timing. Helping someone to focus on the positives and what is going well can expand their problem-solving ability and lift their mood. What feels important is that we have listened to the other person and have tried to understand where they are at first.

The Co-Ruminator

What is Their Intention?

The co-rumination habit is very human. When we say, "Me too, let me tell you how bad things are for me," we are trying to connect, to show the other person that they are not alone, to show how we are the same. Obviously, there are also people who just enjoy talking about themselves – we all have friends like that.

What Might They Say?

The Co-Ruminator might be heard to say, "Me too. Let me tell you how my story is like yours…" or "I know exactly how you feel, let me tell you all about what is going on with me."

What Might the Unintended Consequences Be?

It feels good to know that you are not alone. The challenge with co-rumination is that you can leave the conversation feeling no better, or even worse. You still have your own challenges and now you also have someone else's situation playing on your mind. The conversation also hasn't given you the opportunity to identify any useful steps forward.

When Might this Strategy Be Appropriate?

I don't know about you, but I've always loved a bit of co-rumination on a Friday night with a glass of wine, chatting with my friends about our love lives. Sharing the fact that we've had similar challenges in the past can also be helpful when someone is on the road to burnout. It's more about how much we share and what we say next. It can absolutely be helpful to say, "I can see how tough it is for you – I've experienced some similar challenges before. Tell me more about what's going on with you." Responding in this way tells them that they are not alone, and then comes quickly back to trying to understand what's going on for them.

The Avoider

What is Their Intention?

The avoider is doing just that, (often subconsciously) not getting into the conversation. It might be that they are diverting the conversation away from emotions that they don't have the time or capacity to be with. It may be that they feel uncomfortable and don't want to say the wrong thing. Their aim could also be to help us by distracting us from the thing that is causing us pain. Avoiding might be the strategy they use with themselves, when difficult emotions come up, they push them away and push themselves forward.

It might also be because that person is experiencing signs of burnout themselves. They might be feeling emotionally and physically exhausted and feel like they don't have anything else to give.

What Might They Say?

Someone who is avoiding getting into the conversation with you might say something like, "I'm sure it will be fine," "Don't worry about it" or "That's just how it is around here, you'd better get used to it."

What Might the Unintended Consequence Be?

When someone gives you an 'avoider-type' response, you can feel dismissed. It can feel as if your feelings are not seen and are not valid. You might start to question yourself about whether you are wrong for feeling this way. My delegates tell me that when they have received an 'Avoider' response from someone, they are less likely to share how they are feeling with this person in the future.

When Might this Strategy Be Appropriate?

If you don't have the time or capacity in that moment, it is absolutely OK not to open up a conversation that you either won't be totally present for, or do not have the emotional bandwidth to be the person you want to be in that moment. Adding in an empathetic statement and some honesty could help – something like, "My instinct is to tell you not to worry because it will be fine, but I can see how difficult you're finding things right now and I really want to have a proper conversation with you. Can we find some time tomorrow?"

Which 'Traps' do You Recognise in Yourself?

Did you feel a little uncomfortable when you read through any of the descriptions? As I said earlier, there are no judgements here – I absolutely recognise the Rescuer and Happy-Maker in myself. To be honest, I know that I can drop into any of them, but those are the two that would be my go-to if I left myself unchecked.

Slipping into one of these incredibly human response styles is very common – we are doing it all the time. The reason that I teach these is because when someone shares with us that they are struggling, we want to respond in a way that is useful to them. To do this, we need to be conscious of how we might unintentionally not be giving them what they need. We want to be confident that we are responding in a way that is useful, and as free as possible, of unintended consequences.

Here are some reflective questions to help you to identify any 'traps' you might be falling into:

- Which of the conversational traps did you recognise most in yourself?
- What is your intention when you respond in this way?
- What are the benefits to the other person and to yourself of taking that approach?
- What are the costs to you and the other person of taking that approach?
- What will you intentionally notice going forward?

Tweaking Our Behaviour

When it comes to changing our conversation style and changing our ways of responding, I would encourage you to think about 'tweaking' rather than tying yourself in knots trying to catch yourself in every conversation. To start with, just notice what you are doing currently. The more we develop the ability to notice, the greater chance we have of catching ourselves in the future.

What I feel matters most when it comes to the quality of conversations is that we recognise those moments that really matter, and we do what we can to consciously respond to the other person in a way that serves them as best we can in that moment.

It takes practice to notice these opportunities and 'tweak' our behaviour, but the difference it can make means that it more than makes it worth doing. Stopping and thinking, "What does this person need from me?" or even voicing it by saying, "What do you need right now?" can help you to increase the usefulness of a conversation.

WAIT! Why Am I Talking?

As a final offering, I want to share an acronym that my delegates love. The next time someone comes to you with a challenge or to share that they are struggling, instead of jumping into your normal way of responding, try asking yourself to WAIT! before you jump in. Just a little pause can give us a fighting chance to do something different to what we might normally do. In the following chapters we'll explore what you might want to do instead…

5

Asking Useful Questions

Think for a moment about the people who, after having a conversation with them, leave you feeling slightly judged or misunderstood. Or the people who leave you feeling a little bit miffed because they spend all your time together talking about themselves or about surface level topics which leave you feeling a bit empty. What is going on?

In human interaction a lot can be going on. One thing I've experienced time and time again is that the amount and the quality of the questions we are asked has a direct impact on the way we feel during and following a conversation.

I've been struggling a little with loneliness while writing this book. What I've noticed is that as a coach and facilitator I spend a lot of time (mostly online) listening intently to others and sharing ideas, but not talking about myself. These are rich conversations, that I feel privileged to be part of **and** I can get to the end of the day and feel that, although I have spent a lot of time with others, I feel an undercurrent of loneliness because I haven't been asked any questions about myself.

To help me to feel more connected to others I arranged to go for a run and a coffee with a friend this morning. She asked me questions about how I was feeling, and I was able to honestly talk about some of the challenges I am facing in my life. Crucially she didn't change the subject after I shared my initial splurge, she asked me questions which enabled me to go deeper. She empathised and shared some of her own experience without moving the focus of the conversation to herself. Later in the conversation we talked through a challenge she was facing, and I took on the role of asking questions, supporting her to think it through.

What Questioning Says Without Needing to Say It

As a coach, I obviously think questions are pretty cool. What does it implicitly tell you when someone asks you a question?

I'm imagining your response as something along the lines of, "Asking questions shows that I'm interested in you," "I value your opinion" or "I care what you think."

Going back to this morning's conversation with my friend, I can't overstate the positive impact that this conversation had. I felt as if a weight I had been holding had been lifted. Someone understood. Someone asked me questions that made me feel seen, heard and cared for. In being able to also listen well and ask my friend helpful questions back, I feel as if I've been useful too. I have been able to give her a similar gift to the one she gave me. This makes me feel good.

Reflect for a moment on a person in your life who you look forward to meeting up and talking with. How do you leave interactions with that person feeling? Next time you are with them, notice the questions they ask you and how these questions make you feel.

Using Questions as Part of a Coaching Approach

Asking useful questions is a key component of taking a coaching approach. As well as making us feel like the other person is interested in us, being asked questions can help us to think better. When we are feeling exhausted, disconnected and ineffective, thinking better could really help us to work out what needs to change.

When you ask coaching questions, you are also saying implicitly, that you see the other person as someone who can solve their own problems. Believing that people can identify what needs to change, and take action to change it, is an important part of taking a coaching approach. When someone else feels that we have the ability to come up with our own solutions, it can help us to feel that way about ourselves. What is it about questions that helps us to think better?

1. Questions Help Us to Open Up and Connect

Questions, particularly open questions (which require more than a yes/no answer), help us to connect with each other and build rapport and trust. When we go beyond surface level topics of conversation – when we start talking about what matters to us, our fears, our vulnerabilities – we get an even deeper level of connection.

2. Questions Help Us to Get Clarity

If we are feeling tired and overwhelmed, our thoughts can become muddled and messy. We can also lose trust in our ability to work out what is most important. On our own, it can be hard to see 'the wood for the trees' because there are just too many things fighting for our attention.

When we are asked questions, we are required to order our thoughts in some way, to pull out the useful information. Asking someone a question like, "What is within your control to change?" encourages their mind to do some sifting and evaluate different courses of action. Even if the answer is that nothing feels in their control, it opens up a new level of clarity. If nothing is in my power to change, then that realisation might free me up to think about where I want to put my energy.

3. Questions Help to Broaden Our Perspective

I recently asked a coaching client who is retiring in a year and was struggling with their motivation, to imagine that he can travel forward in time to the date of his retirement and look back at the year. I asked him to reflect on what he hopes will make him feel proud. By changing the position in time that he was viewing the situation, he was able to much more easily speak about what he hoped to have achieved and how he wanted to see his team develop.

When we are struggling with stress, we can be 'head down,' focused on the challenges at hand, which can result in us feeling stuck in the middle of our problems. Being asked a question that can lift our gaze and give us a different perspective can help us to see beyond our immediate challenges. Looking at our problem through the eyes of someone else, or from ourselves at a different period in time can help us to think more clearly.

4. Questions Help Us to Work Out What is Really Going On

I see time and time again that the problem that niggles us and consumes our energy is not really the issue. Yes, it's something that needs to be resolved but it's often a distraction from, or a symptom of, a bigger challenge. When I ask, "What's the *real* challenge here?" or "What's the worst-case scenario that your mind is playing out?" it can help someone to get to the challenge below the challenge. For example, they may think that the problem is about their manager micro-managing them. However, when we explore it on a deeper level, they recognise that they have a fear of being 'found out' that they don't really know what they are talking about and are worried about losing their job. It doesn't mean that a conversation with their manager isn't needed, it just helps them to see why it is affecting them so much and they can then decide what most needs their attention.

When we have greater insight into our problems, we have a greater chance of working on longer term solutions that get to the root of our challenges rather than 'twiddling' at the edges.

5. Questions Help Us to Work Through Our Choices

We might feel we have full awareness of the choices we have, but when we start to think them through on our own, we can get hit by reasons we can't move forward or can feel overwhelmed by what needs to change in order to get there. It can just feel too hard.

Having someone to ask us questions like, "What is the first step you need to take?" or "What feels achievable in six months?" or "Who can support you with overcoming that barrier?" can just help us, in a very practical way, to remove some of the internal and external barriers holding us back from moving forward.

6. Questions Can Help Us to Recognise What is Working

When things feel difficult and every day feels like a survival assault-course, we can lose sight of what is working in our lives. When someone asks us a question like, "What is going well right now?" it can help connect us with the positive things in our lives. Research by the positive psychologist Barbara Fredrickson (2011) has shown how increasing our positive thoughts can help us to improve our thinking and our ability to come up with creative solutions.

Questions and Burnout Prevention

Questions can help someone at risk of burning out for all the reasons above. In particular, they can help us to step out of an internal thinking space that has a short-term survival bias and enable us to just lift our heads a little and see the longer-term impact of our current situation. Having someone ask us useful questions also takes our thinking out of our heads. As we verbally articulate our challenges to someone else, it can feel as if the space containing our struggles opens up. Someone showing empathy, followed by a simple and open question, like, "Tell me more" (not technically a question, but an invitation to say more), "What is worrying you most?" or "What do you want to be different?" can help them to shift their thinking towards a way forward.

If we think back to the Job Demand-Resources model of burnout that I shared in Chapter 1, one of the demand elements that can lead to burnout is feeling like you don't have any control. Being asked questions, particularly when they are structured in a certain way (we'll discuss this in the next chapter), can help us not only to identify what is within our control, but as we identify actions and put them into place, it can help us to increase our sense of being in control of our lives. One of my favourite questions when working with clients at risk of burnout is simply: "What is within your control?"

What to Avoid When Asking Questions

If we want to ask useful questions, there are also some things we might want to avoid. I am sharing general suggestions – there are obviously nuances, so feel free to integrate these suggestions into what you already do.

1. Closed Questions

If we ask a yes or no question, we tend to get a yes or no answer. We call these closed questions, and we tend to avoid them (for the most part) in coaching because they don't encourage the other person to open up and talk to us. There are, of course, exceptions to this. Closed questions can be helpful to clarify that we have understood what someone is telling us. In this case, we might summarise what we've heard and then ask, "Is that correct or have I misunderstood anything?"

A closed question at the end of the conversation can also confirm the action or commitment that someone has made. Asking something like, "So, you are going to go and clear your diary tomorrow morning so that you can make a plan for the next six months, is that correct?" can help the other person be clear about what exactly they are going to do.

2. Habitual Questions and Stock Answers

Anyone who has a child in school knows that if you ask, "How was school today?" depending on the age of the child, you get anything from a 'good' or 'fine' through to a grunt or silence. I've tried to be inventive over the years asking, "What was the funniest thing that happened today?" or "What did you learn?" or the classic, "What did you have for lunch?" To be fair, at nine, my daughter can't remember the answer to most of these questions, so I'm not that hopeful of getting much more from her as a teenager.

How do you tend to respond when someone asks you how you are? Maybe your instinctive response is, "I'm fine," or "Not bad" or a version of "Hanging in there!" One of my best friends is Norwegian and she tells me they reply with, "Oppe, og ikke gråter" which translates as, "Up and not crying." As a perimenopausal woman, this really resonates with me.

These stock answers become a habit – an instinctive reaction, rather than an honest response to the question being asked. I now often change, "'How are you?" to "What are you feeling today?" to encourage the other person to give me more than their instinctive response.

3. Leading Questions and Sneaking Advice into the Question

If we are an 'Advice Giver' it can be easy to form our suggestions as a question, leading the person to think specifically about the thing we think they should do. We can also find our judgments sneaking into our questions, when we ask things like, "Do you think that was the right thing to do?" or "Do you think she is jealous of you?"

The longer the question is, the more likely it is that we have snuck some of our advice or opinion within it. When someone has a strong urge to advise or rescue, they might ask something like," Have you thought about what other opportunities might be available to you if you looked for another role?" This obviously is a question; but really, it's advice disguised as a question.

The smaller the question, the less likely it is to be leading, and the more open it tends to be. Asking something like, "What is working well?" or "What options do you have?" are straight forward and don't give away what you are thinking the other person should do.

4. Avoid 'Why'

As a rule, I try to avoid starting a question with 'why.' This is because it can easily sound judgemental. As an example, I might swap, "Why did you do that?" for "Tell me more about the motivation behind that choice."

There are always exceptions when we make rules and in this case the exception is the question, "Why is that important to you?" or "Why does that matter?" These types of 'why' questions can be helpful at cutting to what really matters to a person. Repeating these questions can be even more powerful.

5. Firing Questions at Someone

It goes without saying, but we obviously don't want someone to feel uncomfortable because of the way we are using questions. Firing questions at someone like we are interrogating them or interviewing them is likely to end up with them feeling defensive and to close down rather than open up.

When we take a coaching approach, we are trying to help someone to think better. This means that we need to break away from conversational norms. In Chapter 3, I shared how, when we ask questions that follow our own interest, we are taking the conversation away from where it would have gone if we had just listened instead. We have unconsciously steered it in the direction of our interest. Unintentionally, our question was in the service of our own curiosity or to help us to solve the problem, rather than in service of what that person needed from us in that moment.

Questions can absolutely be helpful AND we need to be mindful about how we use them. Knowing this, I check myself before asking a question. I ask, "What question would most be in service to the other person right now?"

Supporting someone to take their mind somewhere else is not always a bad thing. If someone can't 'see the wood for the trees,' or their mind is going around in circles, then they might be grateful to be supported to go in a different direction. In the next chapter, I will be sharing with you a way of structuring questions in a way that can help someone move from a jumbled-up problem to a first step forward.

Structuring Our Questions

One of the challenges of asking questions is time. Delegates on my courses share that they fear that if they ask someone a question, it could set off a stream of consciousness that sends someone down a rabbit hole that they won't be able to get them out of. Conversations can feel messy and unruly, especially when people are exhausted and stressed.

I shared earlier in the book that when we ask a question that is in our own interest, we can take the conversation in a direction that serves us rather than the other person. When we notice that someone's thinking is muddled and they are struggling to gain clarity, we also have the same 'power' to direct their thinking to a place which could serve them better. By structuring our questions in a certain way, we can help the other person to think better.

When time is a precious commodity, supporting someone to gain clarity on their challenge, to identify what they want to be different and what might be in their power to make this change happen, is a powerful skill to have.

The GROW Model

There are many different coaching models that suggest questioning structures, but I want to keep it simple. If you have attended even a short course about coaching, I'm sure this model will be familiar to you. I won't be offended if any professional coaches want to skip this chapter – granted you can't actually see whether I get offended, but the sentiment is there. Having said that, I find it beneficial to go 'back to basics' and remind myself of the tools I use on 'autopilot' so you are also very welcome to use this chapter as a refresher.

The GROW model, developed by Sir John Whitmore in the 1980s (Whitmore, 1992), was the first coaching model I was taught over twenty years ago and is the one that feels, still to this day, as if it sits somewhere in the background of my mind, influencing the questions I ask in a mostly unconscious way. I appreciate the simplicity of the model and it is the one that I teach on my coaching skills courses because it is relatively easy to pick up and use from day one.

When you use the GROW model, your questions roughly take the structure of:

- Clarifying a GOAL.
- Exploring the REALITY of a situation.

- Considering OPTIONS.
- Deciding on a WAY FORWARD.

In the Resources section at the end of the book, you'll find a link to my website with example questions for each stage of the GROW model. My course delegates print this out as a crib sheet for when they are first starting to use the model.

Let's explore in more detail the four sections of the GROW model.

GOAL

In the GOAL stage, you take a problem that might feel messy and unclear, and you help to pull it into a clearly defined Goal, by asking something like, "What do you want to be different?" It is important that both you and the person you are having the coaching conversation with are clear about what the Goal is before you move on.

It can be tempting to take the first thing you hear and then rush on to the next stage, particularly if you are a person who likes to fix or problem-solve. Instead, spend some time making sure that you have the specific thing that the person wants to work on before you move on.

When you are short of time, it can also be helpful to clarify a Goal for the time you have, which could look like, "I'm aware we only have twenty minutes together – what would you like to leave this conversation with?"

REALITY

The Reality is when it all comes tumbling out. In a standard conversation we get lots of 'Reality chat.' The beauty of getting into the reality **after** defining the goal, is that the reality now needs to relate to the goal. Which enables us to hold a reality 'container' for the other person. This is especially useful if someone tends to go off track. You are able to say, "Bringing this back to the goal you set, is this the most important thing we need to be talking about right now?"

In the reality stage, you ask questions that open things up like, "What is the *real* challenge for you in this situation?" You are helping the other person to look at the challenge from different perspectives. This stage is about helping the other person to understand what is going on. We aren't looking for solutions at this stage, we are looking to help the other person gain greater clarity.

OPTIONS

In this section of the GROW model, we are supporting the other person to lay the foundations for identifying a solution. We support them by helping them to narrow down their next steps.

"What are your options?" is one of my most used coaching questions. There's no fluff. It's a simple question that can help us to take one step back from a problem, raise our eyes a little, and articulate the various courses of action we have. Just asking this question alone can be a catalyst to someone finding a way out of a problem.

The initial answer to the question can also reveal a lot about where the person is at with their thinking. We can get caught in a binary place where we feel we only have two options. If it's a workplace relationship challenge the person might say, "I either avoid them, or have to suck it up and pretend that I like them," or if a person is unhappy in their role, they might say their options are either that they stay and feel miserable or they find another job. Being only able to see two options, especially where neither feel appealing, can contribute to us feeling stuck. A follow-up question that can really help is, "What other options might there be?" or "If I told you that there was a third option, what do you think it would be?"

If someone is struggling to identify what their options are, you might use another of my favourite questions, "What advice would you give a friend or colleague in the same situation?". Often it is so much easier to give advice to other people than it is to ourselves.

WAY FORWARD

The final stage is about supporting the other person to decide what they are going to go away and have a go at doing differently.

I like questions which help the other person to identify small steps that can build positive momentum. A question like, "What's the smallest and easiest action you can take to move towards resolving this issue?" can help someone to identify something that they feel able to do. When we are talking to people who are experiencing the symptoms of burnout, making actions small and manageable is much more likely to build confidence than a big commitment that becomes another thing that they need to do and may send them into overwhelm.

In this stage, it can also help to check a person's commitment to taking the action by asking something like, "How would you rate your commitment to that action out of ten?" If the response is less than 9, then you can explore how you can change the action to make it easier and more likely to happen.

Staying Flexible

The GROW model doesn't need to be used rigidly and mechanically. Although we are generally moving from 'Goal' to 'Way forward,' we can move forward and back in our questioning depending on what we sense the other person needs.

When people first learn to use the GROW model, they report it being clunky, which makes sense because they are having to be much more conscious about the questions they are asking. We are changing conversational habits that we have had for years.

It can help to just pick one question that you want to practise asking and see how that goes and then build on this each week or month. It can also help to print out the list of suggested questions from my website (link in the resource section at the end of the book) and have them handy for when you have a conversation that might benefit from taking a coaching approach. The delegates who attend my coaching skills course sometimes write their own questions, which sound like them, and reflect the types of questions they would naturally ask. This makes it even more likely that they will use them in practice.

I'm hoping that this chapter has left you feeling a little more confident in how you can structure a conversation to support someone to find their own solution. I'm sure that by now you have gathered how much I advocate for asking useful questions. However, I'm also aware that sometimes an approach that it is a little more visual and maybe a little less intense than pure questioning alone can be helpful when we are having conversations with someone that we are concerned might be close to burnout.

In the next chapter I will share a simple tool that I have used with individuals, teams and groups that can get a conversation about wellbeing started.

7

Starting a Wellbeing Conversation

It might feel quite challenging jumping into a conversation with someone about their wellbeing. We might not know where to start or may be concerned about finding the right words. In this chapter, I'm going to share an incredibly simple tool that you can use with yourself or with others, which makes taking small positive steps easier to do.

Again, I want to iterate that I do not believe that we as individuals are responsible for burning out or that it is our fault if we aren't able to stay well. The ideas in this chapter are about supporting you to do things to help yourself and others, whilst also acknowledging that if you are facing high demands and low resources, something needs to change in your environment too. Before I introduce the tool, I want to address the realities of trying to stay well in our current context.

When Deprivation Becomes Normal

Imagine you're in one of those romcoms where you are given a puppy or a small child to look after. After the initial *I don't know what I'm doing so I'm going to walk around with the baby/puppy at arms-length until someone helps me* scene, your character's mind would start clicking into the things that they need to be focusing on (maybe helped by the arrival of the love interest). By the end of the movie, your character is an expert in how to keep the tiny puppy/person fed, exercised, hydrated, safe, stimulated, loved and rested. As the romcom will have demonstrated, bad things can happen if we don't keep on top of those things.

One of the reasons we laugh at characters in these movies is because it's funny to see a grown adult feel so clueless about how to care for a helpless 'being.' And yet, this is the situation we find ourselves in when it comes to caring for ourselves. As adults we develop the ability to cope with deprivation. It's because we can cope without the essentials that a toddler would almost certainly kick off about, we forget that we are an animal with fundamental needs that need to be met. We can push through if we don't get a full night's sleep. We can skip the healthy breakfast and grab a Kit Kat and coffee in the canteen to keep us going. We can swap water for coffee. We can work long hours and fall asleep on the sofa as soon as we sit down to watch a show we love. I could go on, but I think you get the picture.

We might sometimes believe that the needs of others feel more important than our own and we just keep pushing on. Our body and mind might give us little signals that things aren't quite OK. We might find ourselves picking up colds or developing strange physical niggles. Our mind might wake us up early in the morning, or we might start to feel the panic of overwhelm, but we push it all down and focus on getting to the end of the day, the weekend or until our next holiday.

For most of us, it's not that we don't know how to take care of ourselves. It's not that on an intellectual level, we don't know that there is lots of research out there telling us that our 'pushing through' behaviour not only leads to drops in our performance but also can have a long-term detrimental impact on our physical and mental health. We know it; and yet it can still take us reaching a crisis point before we take action.

Why is it So Hard to Stay Well?

Take a moment and ask yourself what gets in the way of you prioritising your wellbeing? I imagine that it is quite a long list with themes around there not being enough time, you not having the energy, or the motivation, or that other things feel more important.

There are lots of people out there on social media platforms who are all too happy to tell you how to increase your resilience or wellbeing. They share their top tips and their 'must do' habits. You might feel inspired for a while but then find it hard to fit their ideas into your life. The problem is that the solutions they are offering are their solutions, the solutions that work for their particular mind and body, in their particular context.

I honestly believe that the problem isn't that we don't know how to keep ourselves well; it's that life (and our own mind) gets in the way. The demands of our work and our loved ones take priority. We get into unhealthy habits during busy periods and find ourselves stuck in negative spirals. When we are head down, just trying to get through the day, it makes sense that we might forget what keeps us well and even if we do remember, it feels as if we don't have the time or energy to do the things we need to do consistently to stay well.

Closing the Stress Cycle

I came across the idea of 'closing the stress cycle' in the brilliant book *Burnout – Solve your Stress Cycle* by Emily and Amelia Nagoski (2019). They present the idea that we often focus our attention on addressing the cause of stress but don't address the stress itself.

With burnout, we are talking about chronic stress. For our ancestors, this would be like having a daily threat of a wolf or a bear thinking they would make a tasty dinner. I'm sure you've heard of the 'fight or flight' response when it comes to stress. When a human experiences a stressor, hormones rush through our body, our heart rate increases, and blood flows to the large muscles preparing us for fighting for our lives or running as fast as we can in the opposite direction.

In the modern world, it's generally frowned upon to immediately react to the stress of receiving an annoying email by either getting into a fight or legging it out of the building. However, the physiological response in the body is the same as it was for our ancestors dealing with wolves and bears. This results in the body being 'soaked' in the hormones adrenaline and cortisol that then have nowhere to go, particularly when we are sitting at our desks. Our body is waiting for the physiological cues that we are safe but because we aren't running from or fighting off our prey, the cues don't come, and the hormones remain. The stress cycle is not complete.

Following this logic, Emily and Amelia state that, "Physical activity is the single most efficient strategy for completing the stress response cycle" They also highlight other activities that can support closing the stress cycle, including taking deep breaths, positive social interaction, laughter, affection, crying and creative expression.

What's extremely interesting about closing the stress cycle is that when we are in a period of high stress, the very things that could help us to avoid burnout are the first things to go. With burnout, we are talking about chronic stress, so the risk of stopping doing these things is that we can speed up our advance towards crisis point.

Intellectually we know that when we stop doing the things that help us stay well, we risk dips in our performance and enjoyment of life. We also know that not prioritising the activities that are good for our physical and mental health can have a long-term detrimental impact. However, in the moment, when our mind is focused on short-term survival, we forget how important these things really are. How can we justify a lunchtime walk or the time it takes to cook a nutritious meal when we have an endless list of tasks to do?

It feels a bit like a 'thinking trap.' Our mind is telling us to do one thing (answer your emails in the evening instead of going to yoga), which feels absolutely logical when you are feeling stressed, and yet this decision means that we haven't engaged in an activity that could help us to 'close the stress cycle.' Intellectually we feel that the time is better spent getting on top of our emails but the more emails we send the more come back. When we wake up the next morning (or in the night), the stress is still there.

The other counterintuitive 'thinking trap' is that the things we stop doing, such as exercise, seeing friends, eating well, engaging in hobbies etc, not only takes away the things that support us to process our stress and emotional load, we are also taking away the things that help us sleep well (at a time when we are already feeling exhausted) and the things that bring us joy.

Let's Not Forget the Role of Context

When it comes to the activities that help us to stay well, it isn't, and shouldn't be, all about what each person in our workplace is or isn't doing. Yes, there is some personal responsibility AND we also need to acknowledge that our modern work contexts don't always help us either. To enable us to engage in healthy behaviours, we need to leave work at a reasonable time, to take breaks and to have time away from meetings and emails. We need to have boundaries.

When I start talking about boundary setting, I can feel myself getting a little angry because boundary settling is another thing which has been firmly put on the shoulders of the individual. We hear things like, "You need to have better boundaries," or "You need to learn to say no." The reasons that we struggle to set boundaries and to say no are varied and complex. Sometimes it's because we are conditioned to please, sometimes because we want promotion, sometimes we are scared of retribution, sometimes it's because we feel good when we help others.

When we put the sole responsibility of holding boundaries onto an individual who is already exhausted and battling with signs of burnout, we are asking them to take on more emotional discomfort. Emotional discomfort that they probably don't have the energy for. This is why I feel passionately that boundary setting should be a 'team sport.' It could be between leaders and their individual team members, or team members collectively talking together about what's getting in the way of them being able to do a good job AND stay well. Having conversations about how we can support each other to hold boundaries is something I'd love to see become a normal part of working life. When we share the responsibility for holding healthy boundaries, we all benefit. It is a practical way that we can help each other to engage in activities that can help us keep burnout at bay.

If you would like to know more (which I hope you will), I have written an e-book which shares a process for collective boundary setting, which you can download from my website (you can find a link in the Resources section at the end of the book).

The Simplest of Tools

I want to share with you an incredibly simple tool that can help you to increase your wellness and create or reinstate healthy habits. It is a great starting point for moving from unhelpful vicious cycles of behaviour that are keeping you stuck in a place of chronic stress, to virtuous cycles, where you build positive momentum, taking you away from a burnout crisis point. It's a tool that you can use as an individual, with a colleague as part of a coaching conversation, or with a team. If you combine it with a conversation about boundary-setting, it's even better.

If you can, I'd love you to grab a pen and paper and write down the following:

- Activities that help you personally to 'close the stress cycle' and process emotions (like talking to friends, exercising, music, writing things down, yoga etc).
- Activities you do purely for the love of them, rather than because they have a productive purpose.

- Activities that enable you to be just you, without anyone needing anything from you.
- Activities that help you to hear your own voice.
- Activities that give you a sense of connection.
- Activities that make you feel proud of yourself.

The Wellbeing Wheel Activity

The best way to tell you about this approach is to guide you through it. Grab a pen and a piece of paper (or an electronic device that allows you to draw) and work through this with me.

Firstly, I want you to write at the top of the page what an increase in wellbeing would give you. What difference would it make to your life? What important things would you be able to do more of? How would you behave differently? Really think about what is most important to you and what, even a small increase in wellness, would enable you to do. Maybe there are people you'd like to spend more time with or a hobby you used to love that you haven't felt you've had time for.

Next, draw a circle on a piece of paper and divide it into six sections, so it looks something like this:

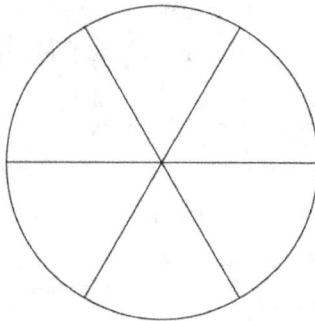

Annotate the circle with six things that, if you did them regularly, would help you to stay well. They might be things you already do, things you've done in the past, or things you've always thought might be a good idea. This could be seeing friends, exercising, reading, sleeping for eight hours, joining a choir etc. Use the list of activities you wrote earlier to help you. Your circle should now look something like this.

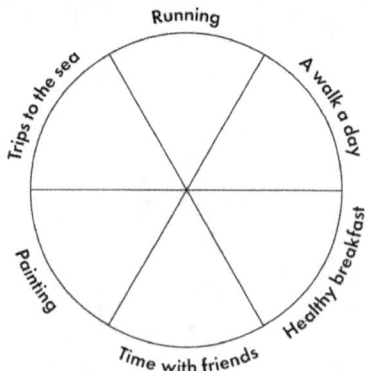

Next, mark in each section a line which represents how much of this thing you are currently doing or have in your life, out of 10. A line on the outside of the circle would be 10/10, meaning that you had as much as you need of the thing. A dot in the centre of the circle would be 0/10 meaning that you are not getting any of that thing. In the example below, I'd like to meet up with a friend once a week and am currently seeing a friend a once or twice a month. Therefore, I have given it a rating of 4/10 and drawn a line to represent that.

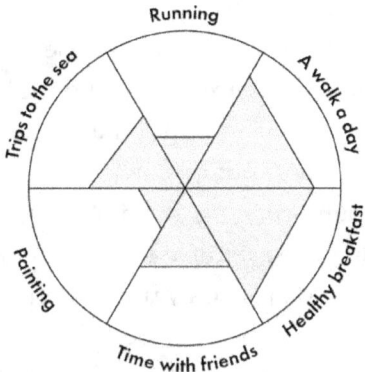

Now choose which section/activity you feel it is most important to focus on first. This may be one you have marked lowest, or the one that feels easiest to tackle first or maybe the section you feel has the biggest impact on the other sections, or for your wellbeing in general.

What could you do differently that would result in a 1-point increase in your score for the section (e.g. from a 4/10 to a 5/10)?

It is worth saying that often people try to be ambitious and jump to a change that would take them to a ten out of ten. We want to change all the sections at once. I call this the 'New Year's Day Effect.' All in one day we decide to change everything at once. We start doing yoga in the morning, we make a green smoothie for breakfast, book a HIIT class for later in the week and swear off alcohol. By the middle of the week we're exhausted from work, hungry from all the smoothy meals and just can't face the HIIT class. We decide that all this wellbeing stuff is not for us, that we have failed or just aren't disciplined enough.

By focusing on taking one step, in one area at a time, we can build our confidence and give ourselves a chance at making lasting change built on a strong foundation of positive habits. For example, when I start thinking about my goals around running, my first thought is that I need to get back to three runs of at least 30 minutes, three times a week. Right now, I am only running once and only for 20 minutes, so I have rated it 3 out of 10. A change I could make to get it to a four out of ten would be to either extend that run to 30 minutes or to add in another 20-minute run. This would help me to build my confidence and protect myself from injury and is much more realistic with everything else I have going on in my life.

Once we have made the first small change and it feels embedded in our life, we can then go back to our wheel and decide where to focus next. It might be another step in the next section, or we might choose to work on another section. What's important is that these small incremental steps build our confidence in our ability to change and start to create positive momentum rather than leaving us feeling like we've failed because we couldn't change everything at once.

Why I Love the Wellbeing Wheel

I am a massive fan of the psychology of habits and behaviour change. One of my favourite behavioural scientists is BJ Fogg. His book *Tiny Habits* (2020) has strongly influenced the tools I use and the questions I ask when I am supporting someone with habit change.

What I love about the Wellbeing Wheel is that it is grounded in some of the key elements of successful habit change that BJ talks about, namely:

- Work out the 'why' behind what you want to change.
- Start with what works for you.
- Limit the number of things you want to change.
- Focus on one area at a time.
- Take one small step forward in this area, choosing something 'tiny' and easy.
- If it doesn't feel easy enough, make it smaller.

What I also took from BJ Fogg's work was the relationship between motivation and ease. When we first commit to a goal we feel high levels of motivation, just like at New Years. When motivation is high, we feel as if we can do difficult things if we just put our mind to it. Then, as we go through our days and weeks, we experience fatigue, and other things come up and our motivation drops. When our motivation is low, the difficult things seem too much, and it is only the easiest things that we will feel we are able to do. Choosing easy things and then building on them incrementally therefore mitigates against the low levels of motivation we are likely experiencing if we are experiencing the symptoms of burnout.

Making the Change More Likely to Happen

Other things I have learnt from the psychology of behaviour change, include:

- Find a way to help you remember to do the thing (like a reminder on your phone or a sticky note).
- Identify whether there is a step before that will make the change more likely to happen (doing an online shop might increase the likelihood of cooking from scratch).
- Often the environment is the easiest thing to change (when I want to eat better, I give away all the crisps and chocolates I have in the house).
- Recognise barriers to implementing your new habit and plan to overcome them (for example, working somewhere different one day a week might help you leave on time because you won't have team members trying to ask questions as you leave).
- Get support from others (like arranging to go for a walk with friends, which increases the likeli-

> hood of you going because you don't want to let them down and will enjoy their company).
>
> - Find ways to reward yourself for implementing your new habit (even things like a tracker where you capture all the times you have done the new habit can feel like a reward to your brain).

Inspired by these ideas, here are some additional coaching questions you can use with yourself or others to increase the chance of the action actually happening.

- What might get in the way of you making this change?
- How might you overcome this barrier?
- What support do you need and from whom?
- Is there anything you could do to make the change more likely to happen?
- What might need to change in your environment in order to make it more likely to happen?
- How will you remind yourself to make this change?
- How could you reward yourself for making this change?

Before I close Part Two, where I have shared the core content of the *Coaching Through Burnout* course, I want to return to Gavin, who you met in the Introduction. Gavin was a delegate on one of the very first *Coaching Through*

Burnout courses in the Autumn of 2022. His story, which he kindly gave me permission to share, can tell you more about the potential positive impact of learning and practicing these skills than I ever could.

8

Gavin's Story

Gavin's story, and stories like them, were the inspiration for this book. Gavin has kindly agreed to share with you the journey he has been on and, just in case you needed a bit more convincing, to explain the specific difference learning these skills has made to him and his colleagues.

Gavin signed up for the *Coaching Through Burnout* course, even though he felt quite cynical about the impact it would have. He shared with me that, luckily, my passion and genuineness shone through. When it was clear that I wasn't just going to present a load of ideas that I didn't really believe in or live – that instead I was going to listen and tailor the course to the delegate's needs – he decided that maybe this course was worth staying for.

Working in the NHS as a Translational Scientist Laboratory Manager, Gavin describes himself as the type of person who people come to for help. He acknowledged that he might have had 'white knight syndrome' as he enjoys 'riding to the rescue.' In the past when a colleague would come to him for help, he admitted being guilty of not really listening to them because he was too busy coming up with a solution.

Gaining a lot of satisfaction from helping people, he tended to be quite parental. If he witnessed people 'falling over,' he would rush over and 'put a plaster on it' and send them back on their way. The interesting thing he noticed was that the people he helped would often come back for help again and again. This had a detrimental impact on his own workload and energy levels. In hindsight, he noticed that although the successes of providing someone with a solution lifted him each time, when the individual came back again for their next 'plaster' he was left feeling drained.

Gavin told me that he came on the *Coaching Through Burnout* course because he wanted to help others prevent burnout – he didn't realise that it would help him to help himself too. Attending the course helped him in the following ways:

- He was able to identify the impact of his 'rescuer' tendency and reflected that in the past, he might have been short-changing people in their own learning by always coming up with the solution.
- The simple acronym WAIT! was a powerful tool to help him to notice that he was jumping in

with a solution, and to just wait and listen instead.

- He started listening with the intent of understanding, rather than listening in order for him to work out a solution.
- He crafted his own questions using the GROW model, which helped him to ask questions that felt authentic.
- Learning about and applying the wellbeing wheel to himself helped him to see the power of making small changes.
- He recognised that he was bottling a lot of things up and was himself experiencing the signs of burnout.

It's nearly two years since Gavin attended the course, and it is still having a positive impact. He now takes satisfaction in not just solving a problem but helping someone solve a problem for themselves. He spoke enthusiastically about how he now gets even more pleasure and pride in watching his team solve their challenges for themselves, without needing to come to him.

Using GROW-type questions has increased the problem-solving skills of both his team and those who come to him for help, which has freed him up to focus on his own work. As an interesting aside, he's found using GROW-style questions with his teenagers has also been highly successful (he's not the first person to say this – one day I might just have to do a course specially for parents).

Since attending the course, Gavin has extended the length of appraisals. Many of his team members are straight out of university and he feels that he has supported their resilience by helping them to problem-solve and increase their confidence in their abilities. He spoke passionately about these skills being just as important as other laboratory skills.

In respect to burnout prevention, Gavin shared that whilst his immediate team has not shown symptoms of burnout, the course gave him a sense of some markers to look out for. Over the last year a few of his extended team members presented with burnout symptoms and he has been able to help them through coaching-style conversations.

Overall, Gavin went from a place of feeling quite cynical about this type of training to being an advocate for taking a coaching approach. In Gavin's words: "You need to try it. Until you do, you won't realise how well it works."

My aim for the previous six chapters was to take you step-by-step through the *Coaching Through Burnout* course. Obviously, you didn't get the benefit of my sparkling company in person, but I hope I've given you some helpful ideas for you to take away and have a go with.

In the next four chapters I want to go a bit deeper. I want to introduce you to the specific approach that I use in my professional coaching practice when I'm working with people who want to avoid burnout. This approach is called Acceptance & Commitment Coaching and its aim is to increase our psychological flexibility, helping us to navigate being human with a little more ease.

PART 3

How Psychological Flexibility Can Help Prevent Burnout

9

Let's Get Flexible

Don't worry, I'm not going to ask you to touch your toes. I haven't been able to touch mine since the early nineties. Instead, in Part Three, I will introduce you to the concept of *psychological* flexibility. Whilst Part Two of the book was about practical foundational coaching skills to support useful conversations, Part Three is where I share the specific coaching approach I take when working with someone who is at risk of burnout (Acceptance & Commitment Coaching). It is also the approach I use for any client who feels as if their mind isn't always on their side or who finds themselves stuck in behavioural cycles that are stopping them from moving forward.

Unlike the previous chapters, this section of the book isn't focused on how you can help other people. This is something for you. Yes, I'm hoping there will be ideas that you can integrate into the conversations you have, building on the skills from Part Two, but this isn't the main focus.

Through sharing ideas that have been helpful to my clients and providing stories demonstrating how my clients applied these ideas in practice, I hope to show you how, with a little more flexibility, we can all face the challenges life throws at us with a little more ease.

If you are reading this as a trainee or professional coach interested in incorporating Acceptance & Commitment Coaching into your work, you can find an e-book on the topic on my website and you might enjoy the podcast I co-host with Dr Rachael Skews called *The Coaching UnpACT Podcast* (link in the Resources section at the back of the book).

Acceptance & Commitment Coaching

At the beginning of this book, I shared how discovering Acceptance & Commitment Therapy (ACT) helped me when I experienced burnout, and how I started to integrate it into my coaching and training practice. When I'm using ACT in a coaching context, I call it Acceptance & Commitment Coaching, because that is what I'm doing (I'm not doing therapy). However, the underlying theoretical basis, processes and practices I use are taken from the ACT literature, so for the rest of the book, I am going to keep referring to ACT to (try) to keep things simple.

What is Psychological Flexibility?

The primary aim of ACT is to support individuals to become more psychologically flexible, which I describe as being able to respond flexibly and consciously to whatever life inevitably throws at us, in a way that reflects the person we really want to be. Psychological flexibility is officially defined, by one of ACT's founders, Steven Hayes, as "The ability to feel and think with openness, to attend voluntarily to your experience of the present moment, and to move your life in directions that are important to you, building habits that allow you to live life in accordance with your values and aspirations." (Hayes, 2019).

Yesterday I experienced a moment of psychological flexibility first-hand. I returned to a car park to find the thing we all dread, that red and white ticket stuck on my windscreen. I had proof from the parking app that I had paid and yet here was a ticket. Typical.

As much as this was an unwelcome surprise, a more welcome one was that I didn't react in the same way I know I have previously. I didn't get frustrated or caught up with how unfair it was, I didn't start panicking about whether I would have to pay it. I calmly took some screenshots of the proof of payment, popped the notice in my bag and made a mental note to email them later.

When we are psychologically flexible, we are able to consciously respond in a way that reflects what's important to us, rather than instinctively respond in a way which isn't helpful to us in the long term. It is through this flexibility that we can also see the choices that we have that enable us to create a rich, full and meaningful life.

We can increase our psychological flexibility by integrating the ideas and practices of ACT into our lives. ACT is a behavioural therapy like Cognitive Behavioural

Therapy (CBT) and is derived from a theory of human language and cognition called Relational Frame Theory (RFT). Luckily, we don't need to get geeky and into the depths of ACT's theoretical background to use it for our purposes.

ACT supports the development of psychological flexibility by (among many other things) increasing our ability to:

- Understand what is most important to us.
- Be willing to take action in the service of what's most important to us, even when it's uncomfortable.
- Be present so that we create the space to make better choices.
- Sit with uncomfortable emotions.
- Notice that we do not need to believe or act on every thought we have.
- Improve our relationship with unhelpful thoughts.

Why Use ACT for Burnout Prevention?

As a psychologist, it is important to me that the approaches I use are evidence based. ACT has an excellent evidence base in therapeutic work and a growing evidence base within organisations and in a coaching context (Skews, 2018). Research has shown that receiving an ACT intervention can result in decreased work stress, increased self-efficacy, wellbeing and goal attainment (Skews, 2018), higher wellbeing and better performance (Bond & Bunce, 2000) and reduced rates of burnout (Spitznagel et al, 2022; Szarko et al, 2022; Towey-Swift et al, 2022).

I have seen time and time again that people who I've been able to support to increase their psychological flexibility are able to think better. Specifically, they are better at noticing what isn't working within their own mind and their external environment, and to work out what is within their control in relation to improving their situation.

Accidentally discovering ACT when I was recovering from burnout was a turning point for me. It took time to integrate the practices into my life. It still takes time. I feel as if working with ACT helped me to create my own user manual. I had been living in a way that although meaningful, was self-destructive. I had to learn another way to live. Improving the relationship that I have with myself has been the greatest gift that ACT has given me. As my relationship improved with myself, so did my relationship with my daughter and my partner. I am by no means perfect, but I am finally a lot closer to being the person I hoped I would be. This came from a foundation of accepting myself as being an imperfect human who is trying their best.

From an ACT perspective, resilience isn't about toughness or just pushing through, resilience is about flexibility, like a tree that bends in strong winds. It is the flexibility to respond to whatever life inevitably throws at us. It is the flexibility that comes when we can consciously respond to a situation in a way that reflects what's important to us, rather than unconsciously reacting in a way that leaves us regretting our actions. It is about being flexible in how we relate to our mind's 'stock' stories about us that can keep us from doing what really matters to us. It is about knowing what matters to us most and recognising where there might be rigidity in our thoughts and emotions which are keeping us from moving towards a life that is more meaningful.

ACT has helped hundreds of my clients and delegates accept their humanness and gain tools to help them to navigate life more skilfully. The challenge of burnout is that we often don't notice it creeping up on us. ACT increases our ability to notice what is happening both inside and outside of ourselves.

Before I jump into the next three chapters, where I introduce three ways to increase your psychological flexibility, I just want to start by sharing six powerful underlying messages from the ACT literature that have been helpful to my clients and to also to me.

Six Powerful Messages from ACT

1. You are not broken

One of my biggest takeaways from ACT has been that so many of the unhelpful things we do are part and parcel of being a human being. Whether it's about being self-critical, being anxious in situations where we could feel rejected, or experiencing strong emotions when something we care about is threatened. This normalisation of the human experience is so important. We are not broken; we might just have some things that aren't working for us in our current context. When we internalise this normalisation of being human, we open ourselves to greater self-compassion rather than trying to continually 'fix' ourselves.

2. You are not your thoughts

Our thoughts are our near constant companion. Until I discovered ACT, I hadn't ever thought about the relationship I had with my thoughts. I guess, on reflection, I thought they were 'me'. My thoughts told me what to remember, what to worry about, what to do. I don't remember ever questioning the intention or the validity of my thoughts, they just were what they were. ACT showed me that my relationship with my thoughts wasn't as simple as I might have assumed. Our mind is a meaning-making machine on a mission to make sense of our lived experienced.

ACT taught me that the fact that I could observe my thoughts meant that they were not 'me.' That my 'thinking mind' was a part of me but it wasn't the whole of me, and it wasn't a voice that I should just accept was speaking the truth or necessarily had my best interests at heart. I'll unpack this more in Chapter 12 because as easy as it is to say, "You are not your thoughts," I also recognise that it is also not an easy concept to get your head around. It's an important idea though, and one that sits at the heart of ACT. Once we are able to see that our thoughts are something that we have a choice about, in relation to things like how intently we listen to them and how we respond to them, then we can start to work on changing our relationship with them. This is particularly true in relation to the less helpful thoughts we experience.

3. You can't just remove thoughts you don't like

Imagine that I've sent you a chocolate cake in the post. You are very excited because chocolate cake is your absolute favourite. When the box arrives, you rip it open, your mouth salivating at the thought of it but what you see in front of you stops you in your tracks, your mouth dries up and a look of disgust takes over your face and you push the cake away. Turns out that I thought it would be really funny to ask the cake shop to pipe 'find the toenail' on the top of the icing. Even though you know that this is one of my terrible jokes, you feel unable to eat the cake. You just can't get the thought that there might be a toenail in it out of your mind. In actual fact, the more you try not to think about it, the more the toenail keeps popping back into your mind. We can't selectively remove the thoughts we don't want and often when we try, we embed the thought even deeper in our mind. It's as if our attention gives it power.

I was reminded of this on my walk this morning. I was lost in my own thoughts and then some beautiful birdsong brought me back into my surroundings. I noticed that as well as the birdsong, I could also hear the roar of the busy dual carriageway. I started getting hooked into thoughts of how nice it would be if there wasn't the sound of cars and I could just enjoy the birdsong instead. I tried to shut out the traffic noise and just focus on the birdsong, but it didn't work. The more I tried not to hear it, the more it was there. *I had to let go of wanting it to go away before it stopped being the only thing I could hear.*

We experience thoughts every day that we wish we wouldn't have. Just like the traffic, we don't have any control over the existence of this 'background noise.' Our attempts to control our thoughts often result in making them louder. We can make a choice to accept our thoughts, let them exist as background noise and attend to something more helpful. I'll go deeper into this in Chapter 12.

4. It is not the thought itself that is the issue, it's our relationship with the thought that trips us up

In my teenage years, I used to sneak into the spare room and snuffle away a piece of arctic roll while my parents watched TV in the room below. I realise that I've never asked them why we had a chest freezer in our spare bedroom, maybe it's best not to. Since the 'arctic roll years,' I have always struggled with my weight and with the belief that I am fat. When I really connect with that thought, when I say, "I am fat" over and over again, what do you think I want to do? Do you think I want to go for a run or eat some lettuce? No. I want to sit on the sofa watching *Love Is Blind* while eating a massive bag of crisps. This statement, "I am fat" is absolute, there is not a maybe about it, no doubt about whether it is true, it is presented as a fact, as a statement about who I am. When we take our thoughts as facts and really connect with them, feeling their truth in our core, something that we call 'fusing' in ACT, we often do not feel motivated to do something that is helpful for us in the long term.

The problem is not the thought itself; the challenge comes from the 'fusion.' When you unpick any of our 'I am' thoughts you start to see that they don't even make sense, and yet they can have a profound impact on our lives. What does 'I am fat' even mean? Yes, my body has fat in it but that's not what the statement is about. Our 'I am' statements are about subjective judgements. "I am not good enough," "I am stupid," "I am a failure." They are fixed stories that we've carried around for years that challenge us because of the relationship we have with them. In Chapter 12, I'll explore with you how you can change your relationship with these kinds of unhelpful thoughts.

5. Get comfortable with discomfort

Humans don't really like discomfort, particularly when it comes to emotions. Think about the enduring messages that you received from your childhood about emotions. Emotions weren't talked about in my family growing up. My parents worked incredibly hard and there was an unspoken rule that you didn't show or talk about emotions because not only did it show weakness, but because it was selfish to draw attention to yourself when everyone was having a tough time. It took me a long time to even be able to recognise and name emotions let alone be able to work out what they are about. This is because I would quickly bury an emotion and then it would pop out at a future time, usually in reaction to something that objectively seemed really small. Since my emotional reactions were so detached from a 'triggering' event, I became quite scared of my emotions because I couldn't understand them or predict when they were going to 'pop out.'

One of the things I have learnt that has helped me most with my emotions is their connection with values. I am angry because something I care about has been threatened or an internal principle I hold has been crossed. I am sad because I've lost something that matters or I'm feeling deep empathy and connection to another being who is suffering. I am scared because I have something to lose that I care about.

I no longer talk about 'negative' or 'bad' emotions and encourage those I work with to do the same. ALL our emotions are fantastic information about what matters to us. The more comfortable we get with the discomfort we naturally feel when we experience uncomfortable emotions, the more likely we are to be able to move through them in a way that enables us to take our emotional data and respond in a way that reflects our values.

There is a term that resonates with me when it comes to emotions, which is the idea of 'sitting with' them. You can apply this idea of 'sitting with' to the whole spectrum of emotions. I was saying goodbye to my daughter this morning and she kept coming back for a hug saying, "Mama, Mama," over and over again and then waved at me for as long as she could when she left. I felt such a warm glow of love, joy and gratitude and I just stood there for a moment letting myself feel it. I can't know how many more of these moments we might have, as she's fast approaching her teenage years. Something told me to just be in the moment.

I work with clients who, like me, have used the strategy of closing down, numbing or 'pushing down' the emotions they found uncomfortable. The problem with this approach is that it's hard to selectively close down emotions. When you shut one down, you risk shutting them all down. I remember reaching a point where I couldn't even remember what made me happy anymore. A participant on a workshop I was running called it, "Having all the joy sucked out" and that is exactly how it feels. If you, a colleague or client finds yourself in this place, then it is absolutely appropriate to have a conversation about therapy. If someone is experiencing a high level of discomfort which is impacting their daily life, then talking to a professional is important. I know how much it helped me when I reached my lowest points.

6. Work out what is most important and build your life around this

Life can feel a bit like supermarket sweep. We've got a limited amount of time, and we need to run around grabbing the right partner, the house, the good job, the 'two point four' beautifully behaved children, the holidays that we can post photos of on Instagram, and so on. We probably aren't sure what we really want out of life at the start, so we grab all the things that everyone else is grabbing, assuming that everyone else must have a better idea of what life is supposed to be about than we do.

In my twenties, I used to paint (pictures, not walls…) before I went to work. I'd rock up at my office job with blue paint splattered up the inside of my arm, mostly hidden inside my shirt. I kept it there all day not just because I thought it made me look interesting; I kept it there as a reminder that I was more than my job. I distinctly remember saying at that time that I didn't want to end up on the corporate treadmill and wake up one day in my early forties asking, "What the hell happened to my life?!" If you didn't skip the intro, you'll know that this is basically what happened, with burnout thrown in for good measure.

I'm not giving away all responsibility for where I ended up but it's easy to see how it can happen. Maybe it has happened to you too. Exploring and clarifying what matters most, and what your own personal version of success is, can help you to start taking small steps towards a life you really want to live. We'll be doing this together in Chapter 11.

Three Ways to Increase Psychological Flexibility

In the following three chapters, I am going to go into more depth around three topics that are core to the ACT approach and come up a lot within coaching conversations:

1. How we can create the headspace to make better choices,

2. Working out and prioritising what is most important, and

3. Dealing with the internal, often unhelpful, chatter in our minds.

When my clients find ways to move forward in these three areas, they increase their psychological flexibility, which enables them to much more skilfully face the challenges in front of them.

Let's start by waking up a frog.

10

Waking Up a Frog

Richard came to coaching because his job was making him miserable. Working as an operations director during the pandemic had left him exhausted and he had hoped that a move to the civil service would improve his work/life balance. Instead, he found himself with a large workload and a challenging boss. His hours kept creeping up and up, and when we started working together in 2023, he was in a place where he could see no way out. He spoke about the extra work he was doing in the evening and weekends as necessary to keep his 'head above water.'

He felt frustrated that he was struggling with the size of his workload and even though he could objectively see that his portfolio was larger than the majority of his colleagues, he felt strongly that if he could just find some coping strategies, then he could make it work.

He shared that the hobbies and interests he had put on hold whilst he worked in the NHS were still on hold and he felt guilty about the time he was missing out with his family. Richard knew that something needed to change but he was so caught up in surviving that he could not see a way forward.

The Myth of the Boiling Frog

You might have heard about the myth of the boiling frog. The story goes that if you put a frog in cold water and then put it on the hob and turn up the heat gradually, it won't notice the water temperature increasing around it and will slowly boil to death. (Nice, I know.) However, apparently, if you drop a frog straight into boiling water it will recognise that it is in hot water and jump straight out.

When I've shared the story of the boiling frog, it has always resonated with the NHS staff I have coached and trained. I don't think it's because they have a particular aversion to frogs; it just beautifully captures how burnout can feel – how we fail to notice the fact we are in a metaphorical pot of boiling water before it's too late.

I don't want to push the metaphor too far but let's just stay here a little longer. Why do you think the frog boiled to death? What's the first thing that popped into your head?

The first thought that came into my mind was that the frog died because **the frog** didn't notice the water getting hotter. With everything I know about burnout and the importance of context, I still blamed the frog! Maybe you did too. Think again – what is the primary reason that the frog died?

The frog boiled to death because a human popped it into water and turned up the heat.

AND my original thought is also true. The frog missed the opportunity to save itself because it didn't **wake up** to the fact that its body was getting hotter. Maybe it was too busy worrying about how concerned the other frogs would be about its sudden disappearance or was ruminating over the reason why it had been picked up and popped into a pot of water in the first place. Who knows. We might also assume that it became acclimatised to the warm water and didn't question when it got increasingly uncomfortable. Maybe it felt powerless and started to believe that that's just what it's like in pots of water.

If the frog had been checking in with its body temperature, it might have noticed that it was getting increasingly uncomfortable. If the frog had been more aware of the power it had to change its context (in this case, leave the pot) then it might have felt able to question its assumption that this is just what happens in pots of water.

The metaphor obviously has its limits. Humans are not frogs. The thing I really want you to take from this is the fact that the frog being boiled alive was absolutely not its fault AND a little bit of **noticing** could have helped that frog to save itself.

Autopilot

The reason that we don't notice the impact that our context is having on us is often because our mind becomes like a pilot who flies the same route repeatedly. It instinctively flicks the switch to 'autopilot' mode.

One of my coachees, Mira, described a typical day for her which I think sums up the idea of being on 'autopilot' brilliantly. Mira described waking up dreary eyed to the alarm, having had a night of broken sleep. She rushes around getting breakfast, getting the kids ready for school, finding various shoes and sports kits that, unsurprisingly, had not been put away in their designated place. Then rushing out of the house, dropping the kids at school, before rushing back home with just enough time to grab a coffee before her first meeting of the day. On a particularly bad day, she would have back-to-back meetings and was lucky if she got to use the bathroom, let alone get something to eat. At least one email a day would cause her to swear and fire off a blunt response. In most of her meetings, she kept her camara switched off so she could do other work at the same time. At the end of the day, after the annoyance of working out what to have for dinner and then the circus of her kid's bath and bedtime, Mira would log back on to work. If it had been a good day, she would crash on the sofa with a glass of wine and a bar of chocolate and watch something mindlessly entertaining.

This kind of day might feel familiar to you. We live in a world where the demands seemingly never end. It can feel like we are on a rollercoaster that we can't escape from. I feel exhausted just reading about Mira's day and I remember the 'Groundhog Day' style exhaustion of living this kind of day over and over again.

When we have so many demands placed on us, it makes sense that so many of our behaviours become habitual. It feels as if there is no time to consciously stop and think about anything (especially what's for dinner). When we are on 'autopilot,' our minds are often lost in the past or the future, thinking about the annoying email you received an hour ago or worrying about how you are going to get the report written when your diary is already full for the day. We are constantly mentally time travelling. I might be physically sitting in Winchester train station for the last half an hour, waiting for a train that had just been cancelled, but my mind has been busy travelling through time and space. I guess it's good that at least one of us gets to travel today!

As I sit here in the station, I have just been gifted with an excellent story of 'autopilot' that made me chuckle. The woman sitting next to me is on the phone telling a friend about the start to her day. She had booked a taxi for 7am and was running late. She glanced out of the window and saw a car in the street outside and proceeded to run out and hop into the back of the car. As soon as she sat down, she realised that something wasn't quite right. The back seat had children's toys on it. It wasn't a taxi at all, it was a man on his way to Sainsburys to do his weekly shop. Just brilliant.

My Three 'Autopilot' Modes

A bit like stress, autopilot isn't necessarily bad. In fact, it's our mind's way of being efficient when there is so much stimuli to process. I have noticed three different modes of autopilot in myself that each have costs and benefits.

Sunday Morning Autopilot

I have a relaxed version of autopilot, where I am just going with the flow and am lost in my thoughts. A bit like a Sunday morning kind of autopilot. I'm getting up, brushing my teeth, making tea, just going through the motions, not consciously needing to think about what I'm going to do next.

I can drop into this style of autopilot when I pick up my phone and start mindlessly scrolling. Time disappears and an hour later I realise I haven't moved and have also purchased a pair of trainers I really didn't need but were such a great colour (damn you Apple Pay for making it so easy). Companies LOVE this kind of autopilot, where seemingly without thinking, we scroll and click and purchase things we didn't realise we needed.

Busy-but-in-control Autopilot

Then there's a 'busy-but-in-control' version of autopilot where my mind is very much focused on forward planning, making sure that I remember everything that needs to be done. I love a bit of efficiency and this 'mode' feels efficient. I'm in the zone, I'm getting s*** done. I'm not doing anything new; I'm doing the things I do well, moving smoothly from one thing to the next, feeling a sense of satisfaction as I switch from one task to the next. I don't need to consciously stop and think about what I need to be doing, my mind is working with me, focusing on what I feel is most important at that moment.

I might not remember to take a break and I'm unlikely to stop and reflect – I'm in action mode. This is the 'mode' I'm often in when my daughter starts to tell me about her ukulele concert or a costume I need to prepare for the next day. I pretend I'm listening, but my mind is focused on things which it believes are more important.

Survival Autopilot

The third mode is more of a rocket-fuelled autopilot. A type of autopilot that has accompanied stressful periods in my life. I notice this kind of autopilot because my mind feels 'fizzy.' I'm jumping from one thing to the next but no longer feel totally in control. I have stress hormones rushing through my body, along with any stimulants (caffeine and sugar mostly) I am using to help to give me a short-term boost of energy.

When I am on 'survival autopilot' mode, my mind's focus is literally about surviving. My attention is directed at dealing with what is in front of me, which means my coping strategies tend to be short-term. I'm not thinking about future Hazel, and I will often choose actions which are not in her best interest.

One of the defining features of this 'mode' is speed. As I speed up, feeling pressured by the demands around me, my mind moves further and further away from the present moment and I am much less likely to be able to notice the 'temperature of the water' I am in (yes, we're back with the frog). The sense of overwhelm clouds my ability to notice what is happening. For me to notice, I have to find a way to slow down time.

How Do We Slow Down When There is so Much to Do?

Slowing down feels like the absolute last thing you want to do when you are under stress. It is counterintuitive but the things that help us to slow our thinking down can be the things that actually help us get stuff done.

When we are in 'survival autopilot' we are constantly reacting to what is thrown at us, as if we are on a tennis court running around picking up the balls we've missed whilst simultaneously trying to hit balls that are being served at us. The reality is that although we feel as if we are getting stuff done, if we reflect on the quality of our thinking and decision-making in these moments, it's easy to see that we aren't thinking well and we tend to make instinctive short-term focused decisions.

To break free, we have to find a Matrix-like way to slow down time (reference to nineties film *The Matrix*, where Keanu Reeve's character is able to slow down time to avoid bullets whilst doing an impressive 'limbo' back bend). If we can do this, we give ourselves a fighting chance to consciously respond to things in a way that reflects what's important to us. If we pause for a moment, we might question why the hell we've been trying to both hit and collect tennis balls at the same time. This decrease in speed might also mean we get the chance to work out what is actually important to us and make decisions that are better for us in the long term.

Please, No More Mindfulness and Meditation

When I think about the practices that have helped both myself and many of my clients to regulate the pace they are going at, my mind is drawn to meditation and mindfulness.

Even though there is some fantastic evidence about the positive impact that mindfulness and mediation can have on our wellbeing, many people have been turned off these practices. They have heard things like, "Feeling stressed? You need to start meditating!" Which can result in a response like; "The issue is that I have three staff members off sick at the moment and we are in the middle of a global pandemic and the staff I have, including myself, are absolutely shattered." Understandably, this person wants to tell their well-meaning colleague where to shove meditation.

These skills shouldn't be seen by themselves as a solution to burnout. It doesn't feel right for them to be offered as a way to cope with an unsustainable environment that is damaging our long-term health. They can absolutely be helpful in helping us to cope with our daily demands, but action must also be taken to improve unsustainable working environments too.

My own experience of meditation has been positive. Reading *Don't Hate, Meditate!* (2019) by the wonderful

Megan Monahan early on in 2020 and then being taught by her, I discovered that meditation was an extremely helpful way for me to process everything that happened in that incredibly challenging time. In contrast to what I used to believe about meditation, I discovered that the aim is not to eliminate all thoughts, so we are left in a state of quiet inner bliss. The skill is to practise noticing our thoughts and letting them pass. Our attention is caught, and we then strengthen our 'muscle of full attention' by pulling it back onto the thing we want to focus on.

I no longer have a formal daily practice; I integrate the skills into my day and take a quiet moment when I need it. Those two years of structured practice helped me through a very emotional time and enabled me to develop the skill of taking a mental step back when I need it.

I see practices that help us to build our ability to be fully present as like going to the gym and doing weights to get stronger. Done regularly they absolutely help us to strengthen our 'muscle' of directing our attention, but it isn't the only way to get strong. Just as day-to-day weight bearing exercises, like a few press-ups in the morning, can increase our physical strength, finding small moments in your day when you practice fully attending to something and then bringing yourself back when your mind inevitably wanders will also help.

Instead of meditation and mindfulness, I talk more about skills that we can build naturally into our days, things like *pausing*, *noticing* and *being present*. These three skills can help us to regulate our pace and absolutely incorporate the spirit of mindfulness, but without the label. What we gain when we strengthen our capacity to be present and slow down is the ability to really notice what is happening around us, and within us, and to make a conscious choice about what happens next. Our thinking improves. We start to see more clearly the power we have to be able to change our circumstances. It feels less like life is happening to us and more as if we have the ability to create and experience a life that truly feels meaningful to us.

The Pause

In ACT we talk about 'present moment awareness.' However, my clients and I talk more about pausing. A pause gives us a fighting chance to notice what is going on around us and within us. It is a moment of wakefulness which can help us to realise that we have a choice about what we do next.

Chloe recognised that she was living her own version of the 'autopilot of survival' at work. She was a doctor working in a busy service, where she rushed from one appointment to the next. She would get to the end of the day fuelled by coffee and with her mind racing. Although she knew she was doing a good job, she also felt as if she wasn't being as present with her patients as she could be, because of all the things that would be whirring around in her mind when she spoke to them.

In our coaching conversation, she walked herself through her day and realised that she had a brief moment of time when a client was getting changed, a time she currently found quite awkward as she hovered waiting for them. Through our conversation she realised that this was the perfect time for her to take a few deep breaths and just slow things down and check in on how she was feeling.

Some other powerful pauses that clients developed were:

- Counting to five before they respond when someone has irritated them.
- Pausing before asking a question, giving the other person space to say something else.
- Taking some deep breaths when they are waiting for the kettle to boil, rather than looking at their phone.
- Not saying yes immediately to email requests.
- Going for a walk at lunchtime without looking at their phone or listening to a podcast.

As you can see above, pauses can be short spaces between something happening and you responding. As with the deep breaths when waiting for the kettle and the walk around the block, they can also be longer, planned pauses that help us to deal with what might get thrown at us later in the day. They can be a moment of reset. A moment of checking in with ourselves.

When we build pauses in and can slow down the pace of life a little, we lay the groundwork for change. We start to see the choices we have. As we make conscious, intentional choices which are different to our habitual way of reacting, we start to break unhelpful cycles and build our confidence in our ability to change things for the better.

Pausing and slowing down our perception of time gives us a fighting chance to move from a place where we unconsciously react to the thing's life throws at us, to consciously responding in a way that reflects who we are and what's important to us.

Noticing

It feels as if pausing and noticing can be a bit of a chicken and egg situation. Pausing can give us the chance to notice; and noticing our current state, or the world around us, can help us to pause. Together they help us to break our autopilot state and become more conscious in that moment.

In Chapter 3, I shared how powerful full attention is in showing someone else that you care. Noticing is a way to do this for ourselves. Just like with the frog, it is through noticing that we start to wake up, giving ourselves a chance to save ourselves. When we are noticing, we are intentionally directing our attention. We can catch ourselves, notice where our thoughts are, notice how we are behaving, notice how we are feeling.

Noticing is often the first skill clients and I work on. I will ask what they notice their mind is saying or how their body is feeling, helping them to strengthen their noticing 'muscle.' Because it is our body that stays in the present whilst our mind is time travelling, it makes the body a helpful tool in bringing us back into the present moment.

Bringing your mind back to the present by focusing on your body can also become a 'circuit breaker' if your mind tends to spiral negatively in certain situations. Focusing on your feet on the ground or on your breath can just be enough to stop your minds spiralling further down. Take a moment now and check in with how your body is feeling. Is there any tightness you hadn't noticed? What speed are you breathing at?

When we focus on our breath, it naturally slows down. When we notice tension in our shoulders, we often roll them. Our mind knows we are experiencing stress because our physiology tells it that a threat is near. If we can notice that we are experiencing a stress response, we can act to 'close the stress cycle'. We can tell our body, "There is no bear," through using our body as a signal. We wouldn't be taking deep breaths if there was a threat in front of us, so by slowing down our breathing, we are showing our mind that there is no threat.

Noticing that we are in a stressed state or 'survival mode' and then taking action to pause and slow down time a little, our mind can step out of its short time survival place and we have more 'bandwidth' to choose what happens next.

Pausing and Noticing in Action

Let's return to Richard, who we met at the start of the chapter. Richard decided that he wanted to start leaving work at 5pm one evening a week, so that he could play with his son in the garden before his bedtime.

I asked him to imagine that it was 5pm and he was trying to leave work and encouraged him to share what was happening in his body at that moment. He said, "When I imagine trying to leave at 5pm I feel very tense in my shoulders, and I feel guilt like a heavy lump in my stomach." He shared that what would happen next is that his mind would say something like, "Just do that email and then you can go." He spoke about the answering of emails being as if it was his mind's way of trying to alleviate the discomfort he was feeling. What would then happen would be that an hour later he would still be there, and he had missed out on the time with his son.

I asked him what might help in that moment, when he recognised the tension in his shoulders and the lump in his stomach. He thought about it for a moment and then decided that he could stand up and walk away from his desk for a moment. He remembered that he had a picture that his son had drawn on his wall and it occurred to him that he could stand up, roll his shoulders and go and look at the picture to remind himself that it was worth feeling this little bit of discomfort because he was leaving at 5pm for a good reason.

It took practice, and Richard wasn't always successful, but by noticing what was happening in his body and mind and noticing the urge to do what he'd always done next, Richard was able to also notice that there was another choice.

In our time together Richard and I also worked on gaining a better understanding of what was most important to him, identifying the time he wanted to spend with his son as an incredibly strong reason why he wanted to change. Maybe it's made you reflect on what might motivate you to change? Excellent, that's where we are going to go next.

11

What Matters Most?

In 2019, Rachel had her arm twisted to become clinical lead for her department. She confessed that she hadn't particularly wanted to do it – she did it out of a sense of duty to her team and her patients. Little did she know that she was about to lead her team through the most challenging time of their careers so far.

I met Rachel in 2021. Her term as clinical lead was nearly over but seeing how challenging the role had been during the pandemic, none of her colleagues was willing to take it on. She felt backed into a corner, joking that the only way she would be able to leave her role was by retiring. Rachel loved her work but had reached overwhelm and was struggling to sleep. It wasn't just her work that was challenging, her home life and the caring roles she played meant that she had reached her emotional limit in both domains. She also led an organisation-wide group that was working on a topic that was important to her and was a key figure in a national professional body.

Things felt hard in her clinical lead role. She felt as if she couldn't escape people asking what to do or looking to her to resolve their problems. She acknowledged that she could become agitated in meetings and felt as if she wasn't being the version of herself she really wanted to be. She felt as if everything was a priority, that everything had to be done, and that it was her responsibility to do the bulk of it. She had lost connection with what mattered most and was struggling to even imagine how things could ever be better.

What is *Really* Most Important?

What behaviour in other people really winds you up? If you find answering that question cathartic, why not write a list of all the behaviours you experience from other people in a given day that 'presses your buttons' and causes you to mutter under your breath.

Knowing what behaviour annoys and upsets you in other people can be a great starting point to discovering the core values you hold and is one of my favourite ways to start a conversation about values with my clients. If you reverse some of those words or ask yourself what this 'niggle' tells you about what's important to you, then it can be a helpful way to start you thinking about your values. If lying bothers, you it might suggest you value honesty, if it's selfishness that 'gets your goat' then maybe you value generosity or empathy or altruism or service.

Values are the principles that we live our life by. They are the personal qualities that, above all others, it feels important that we embody. When we see what feels like the opposite of these values in other people, it's like a 'flashing red light' that goes off in us (or, as the kids say, a 'red flag').

Values are often described in individual words, like honesty, creativity, connection etc. We can look at a list of values words (for an example list, see the link to my website in the Resources section at the back of the book) and feel as if many of them are qualities we want to be known for. Our core values are those that feel so obvious to us that, if questioned as to why they are important, we would respond with a 'just because' or 'I can't imagine that quality not being important to me.'

I say that if we were cut in half then these are the words that would tumble out. A slightly less gory idea I heard once was to imagine that we were a stick of rock and our values were the words we see would inside (if you haven't had the pleasure/pain of eating a stick of rock, it is a sickly long solid cylinder of a sweet we get at the seaside in the UK, which has words running through the entire length). If you are keen to get going and start exploring your values, there is a link to a worksheet in the resources section at the back of the book.

Values as a Compass

A helpful metaphor for understanding values is that of a compass. Unlike goals, which give us a specific destination to strive towards, and a sense of achievement when we have reached it, values are more like a direction of travel. You don't respond to a call from a friend who needs your help, and then sit back and relax knowing that you've achieved 'friendship' and never need to do it again. To live the value of friendship you need to be showing up regularly in the spirit of friendship. That doesn't mean that you need to do it 100% of the time (we'll talk more about 'holding lightly' later) but it is something that, if it is absent in your life, will leave you feeling disconnected from who you feel you really are.

In our modern world, we are directly and indirectly told what is important and what our lives should be about from a very young age. Some of this comes from our family, some from school and some from books, magazines, social media and organisations who are trying to sell us products or services. It can be hard to work out for ourselves what is truly important to us because there are plenty of people ready to tell us what we *should* be caring about and where we *should* be putting our time and money. Whenever I hear a 'should' an alarm goes off in my head. 'Should' is a word to notice and be curious about. It often means that there is a difference between what we *want* to do and what we perceive other people think we *should* do.

When we make the time to work out what is important to us, we start to notice these subconscious influences on us and start to be much more conscious about what *really* is important to us. We start to identify what a successful life is on our own terms, which is usually what makes it feel meaningful, rather than a pure achievement-based version of success.

From a Human 'Doing' to a Human 'Being'

Because values are about 'being' rather than 'doing' they help to connect us back to ourselves as human beings. When we are caught in a place of 'busy' or 'survival' it can feel as if we are just 'doing machines,' whose value is about what we've achieved or what we've done for others. Values can help us to step back and see ourselves as being enough, just for being us. When I look at my nine-year-old daughter I see this in action. She is more than enough just for being the fun, courageous, creative and kind person she is. She doesn't need to achieve anything for me to be proud of her. If only it was as easy to feel the same way about myself.

Throughout my life, my belief that success was about achievement, particularly in respect to the job I had and the qualifications I gained, led me on a very narrow path of putting these achievements above everything else. I reached my early forties feeling as if I didn't really know who I was or what was important to me. The process of defining my core values (learning, love, creativity, freedom and service) helped me to see myself beyond what I had achieved. The idea of what a successful life was for me, was starting to take on a different form. I also started to really own my role in defining what the life I wanted to live looked like, and I could see more clearly the agency I had, to be able to make it happen.

Being Intentional with Values

Values are incredibly powerful when we use them intentionally. I worked with a client who was struggling to find her voice in team meetings. She identified that one of her values was 'Community' and that, for her, one of the things that value meant was representing the people who did not have a voice in that leadership forum. Connecting to this value before and during the meeting helped her to be less concerned about her nervousness about getting it wrong and more focused on the people she was giving a voice to.

In my own life, when I have gone through tricky periods, I have found that writing a few lines about my values, and the particular value I planned to intentionally bring into the day, incredibly powerful. Often it feels like our minds are wired to just notice the bad stuff or the things that we haven't done as well as we would have liked. When I am consciously bringing values into my day, I find that I notice how my values are playing out more and I end up feeling more connected to myself.

In her book *The Upside of Stress* (2015), Kelly McGonigal shares findings from multiple research studies exploring writing about values. She talks about values being one of the most effective psychological interventions ever studied. She says, *"In the short term, writing about personal values makes people feel more powerful, in control, proud, and strong. It also makes them feel more loving, connected, and empathetic toward others. It increases pain tolerance, enhances self-control, and reduces unhelpful rumination after a stressful experience."*

McGonigal goes on to share that the long-term impact of writing about your values, even once, for ten minutes results in multiple benefits months later, including improved mental health and reducing visits to a doctor. That blows my mind a little, and I'm already a fan of values. Just writing about our values for ten minutes can have a lasting positive impact. It's one of the reasons why values work forms an essential part of the work I do with my coaching clients – it's impactful and efficient.

Two Sides of the Same Coin

An incredibly powerful function of values is that they provide us with a starting point to understand why we have been emotionally affected by something or someone, particularly if we are having trouble letting that thing go. There is a metaphor in ACT which talks about values being like a coin. On one side of the coin is all the helpful 'stuff' that comes with living a particular value and on the other side of the coin is the discomfort that also accompanies it. Say you have a value of fairness, on one side of the coin there are all the positive qualities that a fair person holds, and on the other side there is the pain, and all the accompanying uncomfortable emotions, that come when things happen which don't feel fair, or fairness feels threatened. When talking about values I say to clients:

> "When we choose what we care about,
> we also choose our pain."

Accepting this idea can be incredibly liberating. Those sensations we might call 'negative' emotions suddenly have something to tell us. If they are connected to one of our values then they are telling us that something that we care about is being threatened, trampled on, or ignored. This helps us to reframe our emotions as a form of values-based 'data' that we can get curious about.

It also opens the door to choice and agency. Sticking with the metaphor of values as a coin, I will ask a client whether they would like to give their values 'coin' to me. This would mean that they no longer feel the uncomfortable emotions, however, they would also no longer care deeply about the value and would not get any of the benefits of holding that value. I have not met anyone yet who is prepared to give a core value coin up.

The question then becomes, "How will I live with this discomfort?" For the person with a core value of fairness, their personal version of discomfort is living with being affected by things happening that feel unfair. Knowing this can help them to expect strong emotions around unfairness. It can help them remind themselves in that moment that they are angry or upset because they are a person who really values fairness. They are experiencing emotions because something matters. Then, they can move into more of a self-coaching place where they might ask themselves what is within their control, what they need or maybe what their options are.

What I witness time and time again is that the identification of core values, and the recognition of the emotional discomfort that comes with holding those values, is a powerful force in helping us to change our relationship with our emotions and can help us to widen our perspective when something or someone has really 'hooked' us.

A few years ago, I coached Caroline, a GP, who had changed specialities several times in her career. Her mind liked to tell a story about her being 'bottom of the pile' in terms of her career. It told her that she should have been further forward and compared her less favourably to her peers who had stuck with one specialism. When she connected with this story and treated it as being true, she felt a sense of shame that she wasn't good enough. In response to this feeling, she would often retreat from her colleagues and isolate herself.

Caroline identified that she had a core value of growth. We spoke about how it can be helpful to identify the specific discomfort that someone with a core value of growth was going to have to live with. She was able to recognise that she had repeatedly made career choices which put herself into situations where she felt 'bottom of the pile.' To grow, she had to put herself in situations where she had a lot to learn. She concluded that it was perfectly natural that her mind would look around and grow fearful because others seem to know what they are doing, and she felt she did not. She recognised that it would be strange to seek out opportunities for growth and never experience any kind of doubt or discomfort.

Noticing that her mind's 'bottom of the pile' story was her personal discomfort that accompanied periods of growth helped her to understand and expect the discomfort. We then worked on strategies to change her relationship to these thoughts (using methods I will share in the next chapter).

Holding Values Lightly

On many occasions, the discussion with clients has become about how they might **care deeply and hold lightly.** I've noticed this phrase come up repeatedly in my work and I feel it epitomises what a healthy relationship with our values feels like.

When we care deeply and hold lightly, we are in a place where we recognise our values and accept both the helpful bits and the uncomfortable bits. We intentionally look for opportunities to live that value and we are also aware of what it can look like when we hold on too tightly to a value.

I want you to imagine that you have been given a baby chick to hold. Take a moment to actually hold your hand in the position you would hold a chick in. I'm guessing that your palm is facing up and your fingers are gently curled. Uncurling the fingers totally would risk the chick falling off, which wouldn't be pleasant. Curling your fingers in tight would result in a potentially even less pleasant outcome. If you're still with me, you'll have worked out that our values are the chick. We want to hold them lightly: not so lightly so that we disconnect from them, and not so tightly that we squeeze the life out of them.

Values and Our Relationships with Others

When I have my eyes tested, the ophthalmologist puts different lenses in front of my eyes, and I tell her which one allows me to see best. A or B. A or B. A or B. Our values are like the lens that we can see the world most clearly through. The challenge of this is that other people see the world through different lenses, yet we can easily assume that we are all wearing lens A. So many of the challenges my clients have with other people have a values component to them. We assume that what is important to us is equally as important to someone else.

This reminds me of a client who was struggling with her relationship with her manager. She held a value of honesty and had witnessed him telling different things to different people. He had also withheld some important information from her. She decided that he was dishonest and just couldn't get past this. She had started to avoid him and did not feel she could trust him, which was impacting both her ability to do her job well and her future career prospects. My client didn't want to care any less about honesty; that wouldn't have been her being her. What she needed was to find a way to hold honesty more lightly to have a healthier relationship with her boss.

We explored the reasons why humans aren't always honest. She reflected on other relationships she had where she had been able to accept less than 100% honesty and how she had done that. She also did some work on what was OK and not OK around honesty for her, which helped her to have a conversation with her boss about what was important to her in their relationship.

Recognising that other people have different core value sets to us, and taking the time to understand what their values are, can transform relationships. Saying things like, "I can hear that respect is important to you – tell me more about what that looks like for you," can be a game-changer in building connections during challenging conversations. It signals that we have seen what is most important to the other person.

Values and Burnout Prevention

When we are experiencing the symptoms of burnout, it can seem logical to stop doing the things that feel non-essential. We stop seeing friends, attending choir practice, going running, getting outside for a walk at lunchtime. Our focus becomes more and more narrow, we just need to try and keep the 'wheels on the bus.' The problem with this strategy is that, not only do we lose many of the ways we were processing our stress, but we also have less opportunity to live our values. It makes sense that we start to feel less 'whole.'

At a recent burnout prevention workshop, a participant described burnout as feeling like a 'joy vacuum.' I really connected with this, and it reminded me that not only do values help us to understand our strong uncomfortable emotions, they also help us understand the more pleasant emotions that we experience. If we have a value of connection, it feels good to be doing something with others. If we have a value around 'nature,' being outside can bring us comfort. You get the picture.

Identifying our core values and then working out small ways that we can get a bit more of any neglected values in our lives can help us to reconnect with being a whole person and help to increase the amount of pleasant emotions we experience.

The other area where values can be helpful in burnout prevention is related to the idea I spoke about above, where values help us to understand strong and uncomfortable emotional reactions. Values conflicts, particularly those around fairness have been shown to increase the risk of burnout. When we can identify the reason behind a strong emotion, we are better able to see where our control lies.

One of the three symptoms of burnout is cynicism and detachment. I have seen time and time again clients experiencing a values conflict within their workplace, which eats them up, and understandably one of the ways they try to protect themselves is to create some psychological distance between themselves and their work.

NHS staff have spoken to me about the daily pain they experience because they can't fully live their values due to limited resources. They often take that pain, bury it deep, and just try and get on with it. In the short-term this feels better than feeling uncomfortable emotions every day. The challenge is that this burying starts to create distance between them and the work that they deeply care about.

They are left knowing that they DO care but feeling that they must find a way to not care in order to survive.

Identifying core values can be a great starting point in enabling us to accept our difficult emotions, expect them, and then work out how we can best live with them or act on them before we end up in a place of cynicism and detachment.

Let's return to Rachel, who we met at the start of the chapter. Rachel was on the cusp of a burnout crisis point when we started working together. After defining her values, Rachel decided to stop doing one of her voluntary roles, a decision that helped her to feel lighter. She started a reflective practice of writing about her values on her non-working days which helped her to step out of 'survival mode' and to ask herself what she wanted to get out of the things she was doing.

Rachel decided that she wanted to do the roles she did well, rather than keep holding onto the belief she had when she was younger, that she had to be able to cope with everything and not admit defeat. Instead, she wanted to do what is right for her now. She also redefined what 'being OK' meant, so that it was about feeling happy and well, not just 'not too awful.' She was clear that she wanted to look after herself so that she wasn't just managing to get by, she was enjoying life again.

She started a practice where she would notice the tightness in her body, which signalled when she was getting overwhelmed, and would ask herself, "Is this how

I want to be?" and "How does this fit with my values?". This supported her to take a step back and focus on how she could be the person she wanted to be in that moment.

Defining Our Core Values

Hopefully I've intrigued you enough about values that you want to start exploring them for yourself and to integrate them into your conversations with others. In the Resources section at the back of the book you'll find a link to a worksheet on my website. I encourage you to find some quiet time and start the process of identifying your values and use the reflective questions on the worksheet to explore how your life could be enhanced through working more deeply with your values.

The Evolution of Our Values

When we are exploring our values, we are asking ourselves what is most important to us. This is a big question to answer and is also an answer that could evolve over time. It's helpful to have a first stab at identifying our values, and then sit with them for a bit and see what we notice.

It can be helpful to come back regularly to your core values and check in with what feels most true to you in relation to your current circumstances. I find it helpful to have at least a quarterly check in, reflecting on the period ahead and the values that I want to be connecting with most in that period.

What Next?

Once one of my clients has a core value set, I start to explore what these values can tell them about the challenges they are facing. We explore whether some values have been getting more 'airtime' than others and which values they may need a bit more of.

Values can help us with many challenges we face, including making decisions about our career, changing a habitual behaviour or improving a relationship. Values also help us to define what a meaningful life looks like for us, so are helpful when we are redefining our idea of success or identifying our purpose. In the Resources section at the end of the book, I have included a link to a list of follow-on values-based reflective questions that I use with clients, depending on the challenge they are facing.

It is often the case that the wise voice inside us, the voice that knows what truly matters to us, is drowned out by internal chatter. This chatter can be critical and keen to grab our attention. To more easily hear our wisest inner voice, and to live a life that reflects our values, it can be beneficial to find ways to reduce the impact of this inner 'noise.' In the next chapter we're going to go even further – I'll share some ways that we can befriend our most critical inner voice.

12

Befriending Our Inner Critic

In our first coaching session, Kerry shared that she had recently moved from a role that she had worked in for years and was very confident and comfortable in, to one in a slightly different field, where she had lots to learn. Although the challenge of the new role excited her, her work environment was difficult, and she came to coaching feeling vulnerable and exposed.

Kerry had been getting positive feedback but had an enduring concern she wasn't good enough and was worried that she would let people down. She spent a lot of time worrying, particularly about the fact that she felt bad sending work to her manager to get it checked before she sent it out. Her role also included delivering training to staff, which she found incredibly stressful and, even though she enjoyed doing it at the time, would be consumed with fear about making a mistake before the session.

She came to coaching because she wanted to stop doubting herself so much and wanted to be able to believe the positive feedback she received. She recognised that the fear she faced daily, both at home and at work, resulted in her holding herself back from fully living life, and she didn't want to live like that anymore.

What are Your 'Records on Repeat'?

In the 'good old days' before music streaming, I remember waiting with anticipation for a tape or CD to be released and then rushing to WH Smith or HMV to buy it before it sold out. Once I got home, I'd lie on the floor and listen to it on repeat. Alanis Morrisette's *Jagged Little Pill* stands out in particular. I still remember a sense of panic when my Sony Walkman made that awful 'I've chewed up your tape' sound and I'd manually wind the crumpled tape back in, hoping it still sounded OK. When I hear tracks from *Jagged Little Pill* or Oasis's *(What's the Story) Morning Glory?* they take me back to very specific times in my life. I remember the lyrics better than I remember anything I might have been studying at school. It's as if these albums made their way into the fabric of my identity. They made me feel certain ways. They became a part of me. In much the same way that the lyrics of these songs are 'burnt' into my brain, there are thought patterns and stories that I tell myself about myself, that feel stored in my mind in much the same way. Some of them are helpful and many are not-so-helpful. These not-so-helpful stories have been there a long time, and just like the song lyrics from my youth, they continue to make an appearance on a surprisingly regular basis.

What are the unhelpful thoughts that are like a 'record on repeat' in your mind? Whenever I work with a coaching client, I ask a question like this. I want to help my client to recognise their thoughts as being separate from the part of them that notices them, and to gain a better understanding of the habitual thoughts that narrate their experience of life.

The Inner Critic

A particular pattern of unhelpful thoughts is often called the Inner Critic. The idea of the Inner Critic – that not-so-lovely voice inside your head that likes to remind you of the mistakes you've made, predict the things that you're going to mess up, and tells you in many different ways that you are not good enough – is one of my favourite topics.

Selfishly this is because my own Inner Critic has been an enduring companion in my life. It mostly stays inside my head, saying things like, "What if you make an idiot of yourself?" or "Look at all those people who are more qualified or more successful than you". Sometimes its words are so loud that they pop out of my mouth. I clearly remember walking along a pavement in a town centre after delivering a presentation and, "You just made a tit of yourself," popped out of my mouth, scaring several people who were unlucky enough to be within earshot.

Avoiding embarrassment is central to my Inner Critic's concerns. If you were a teenager in the nineties, you might remember the craze of wearing green foundation. As a teenager I used to go red at the drop of a hat, something my schoolmates found highly amusing, so every morning

I would cake myself in green foundation, hoping to cancel out the embarrassing red glow. Unfortunately, if I wasn't red with embarrassment, I inevitably walked around looking like Grotbags (another nineties reference – she was an ugly green witch on kids TV). Secondary school was not a great time for me.

The other strong message that came from my school years was that failure was not OK. I saw how proud my Dad was when I got an A for an exam or assignment. Academic achievement became my 'thing.' When I received a B in my English GCSEs my mind told me, "You've failed." When I received a 2.2 in my first degree, I couldn't even go to my graduation. I had to do another degree and get a First, just to prove that I wasn't a failure.

I walked into adulthood with two strong internal critical narratives: "Don't make a tit of yourself" and "Never fail." Every time I did anything slightly embarrassing or failed to reach my own ridiculously high expectations, I would internally shout terrible things at myself.

It is undeniable that this voice drove me to achieve things I am proud of, but it was a painful way to motivate myself. My mental health suffered because of it. Like many people, I tried ignoring it, rationalising with it, arguing with it and telling it to f*** off and leave me alone. I feel like these strategies worked as well as they might work with a toddler; the more it felt unheard, the louder it got. I recognise now that I was trying to control it in a way that ended up with it having more power over me.

The Inner Critic and Burnout

It's easy to see how the combination of a critical inner-voice and a stressful context can exasperate burnout symptoms. If we are feeling tired, ineffective and disconnected it gives our Inner Critic lots of ammunition. We can find ourselves filling in the gaps in what other people have or haven't said. We can feel more sensitive to perceived criticism from others. We can tell ourselves that we are letting people down if we need to stop and rest.

We do not feel safe in a place of chronic stress. We are in survival mode, head down and focused on maintaining some sense of control. It makes sense that our mind wants to motivate us into action. If being tough on ourselves and pushing through has worked before then why not in this situation?

The problem with using our critical voice to motivate us when we are experiencing the symptoms of burnout is that, not only does it make us feel worse, it can also result in us reaching for coping methods that can exacerbate our symptoms and speed up our advance towards crisis point.

We feel crap, so we look for things that distract us or numb our feelings. The glass of wine in the evening becomes a bottle, which disrupts our sleep even further. We comfort eat or grab snacks on the go rather than eating proper meals and end up feeling depleted and sluggish. Our mind might tell us that we don't have time for exercise, hobbies or seeing friends and we start to feel more isolated and disconnected. Our rest time involves crashing out to watch TV and then reaching for our phones as a way to distract us from our uncomfortable emotions.

There is absolutely no judgement about any of these things. I have spent years learning about burnout and I know that the way I try and cope with my uncomfortable thoughts and emotions usually results in short-term release but is no help to me in the long run. However, I do still sometimes do these things in times of high stress – I'm still human.

I saw the Inner Critics of the NHS staff I coached through the Covid Pandemic, causing problems in many ways. I introduced you to Kerry at the start of the chapter. Kerry's mind was bombarding her with worrying thoughts, making her doubt herself and the positive feedback she received. Her context was challenging and the way her thoughts were behaving was also contributing to her questioning whether she was able to stay well in her current role.

What I noticed again and again is that when my clients started spending less energy trying make their unhelpful thoughts go away, they had more energy to focus on improving the things in their environment. They were then able to use the energy that they did have to take small and helpful steps away from burnout.

I've learnt that our environment/context is key in burnout **and** our thoughts impact the relationship we have with our context, which can drive our behaviours in unhelpful ways. There will be so many aspects of our context that we cannot change, however our relationship to our thoughts is something we **can** change.

You are Not Alone

"'Write on the sticker the worst thing you say to yourself, then stick it on your top and walk around the room." This was not what I had signed up for. It was 2018 and I was attending one of my first ACT training courses with hundreds of ACT therapists from across Europe. As one of the only non-therapists in the room, I was worried that if I was honest about what I wrote on that little white sticker that I would be 'outed' as someone who really needed therapy. My brokenness would be on display for all these therapists to see. I nervously scribbled down, "I'm a failure," and took a deep breath.

Everyone stood up and slowly started rotating around the room, glancing from labels to faces. I was shocked as I saw label after label of hurtful thoughts. "I am unlovable," "I am disgusting," "I am a fraud," "I'm not good enough," "I'm lazy."

As I looked into my fellow participant's eyes I saw compassion, encouragement, and a deep knowing. It was the closest I've ever got to a sense of common humanity. There we were, sharing our worst thoughts about ourselves and living to tell the tale. Looking across the room it suddenly dawned on me that therapists must have therapy as part of their training, and then engage in ongoing training and supervision. If the people in this room hadn't been able to get rid of the terrible things they could say to themselves, then what chance do the rest of us have?

It was such a beautiful, vulnerable and moving demonstration that the Inner Critic was a very normal, human voice to have. Having an Inner Critic doesn't mean that I'm broken or that there was anything wrong with me for having it.

What are Our Minds Trying to Do?

Let's return to the green-faced, academically driven, teenage me. Why was embarrassment and failure such a big deal for me?

What I learnt as a teenager was that embarrassment led to potential rejection from my peer group and that academic success gained me approval from my caregiver. For early humans, rejection from their group was a serious business as it could lead to isolation from the tribe, which was a life-threatening occurrence. Looking back, it therefore makes sense that my mind would want to warn me about embarrassment and keep me on-side with the person providing me with food and shelter.

In ACT, every behaviour (including internal behaviours like thoughts) has a function – it happens for a reason. I realised that criticising me was my mind's twisted way of trying to keep me safe. I say to my coaching students: "Your mind's primary focus isn't on living a full and meaningful life; it's primary focus is your survival. It is trying to keep you safe." It seems illogical how our minds often seem to try and make us safe by saying things to us which make us feel less safe and cause us pain. However, knowing this can help us to start the process of living more easily with these thoughts.

Defusing from Unhelpful Thoughts

In Chapter 9, I spoke about hearing the sound of a dual carriageway on my walk and how it was only when I stopped trying to make the sound go away that it stopped annoying me. This reminds me of the metaphor of quicksand. As with quicksand, the more we struggle against our uncomfortable thoughts, and try to push them away, the deeper down we go and the more 'sucked in' we get. It feels counter-intuitive but it's only when we stop struggling that we have a chance of finding a way out.

I love seeing the liberation that my clients experience when they stop trying to get rid of their unhelpful thoughts and start to recognise them as something that makes sense in the context of surviving as a human being. This knowledge in itself is incredibly helpful; however, it doesn't stop the thoughts coming. If we have developed a habit of instinctively reacting to these thoughts in an unhelpful way over a number of years, we are going to need a strategy to help us to live with them in a way that doesn't negatively impact us.

I shared in Chapter 9 that the challenge with thoughts isn't the thoughts themselves; it's when we get 'hooked' or 'fuse' with them, treating the stories they tell us as facts. When we do this, the behaviours that come next are not helpful behaviours – they are short-term coping strategies (like the way I described responding to "I am fat" by watching reality TV and eating crisps). Although they might help us in the short-term, there can be long-term costs.

One of the ways that we help ourselves to live more easily with our thoughts is to learn how to create some distance from them; enabling us to have a bit more choice about how we respond to them. In ACT we call this 'defusing.' When we can 'defuse' from our thoughts, we have more flexibility about what we do next. Firstly, we need to notice the recurring thoughts that tend to trip us up and then, when they pop up, we need to notice that we have been 'hooked.' Once we've developed this skill of noticing these unhelpful thought patterns, we have a fighting chance of changing what happens next.

The best way for me to describe my favourite 'defusing' technique is to walk you through it. It might feel a little uncomfortable at the start but stay with me (obviously with the caveat that you ensure that you are in a safe space and to choose a thought that isn't too painful).

Firstly, I want you to think about an 'I am' statement that your mind holds about you, that you don't particularly like. Say that 'I am' statement to yourself ten times. So, for me I'm saying, "I'm a failure," over and over again in my mind, ten times. Notice how this feels, really tune in to the sense of this statement.

Now I want you to change it to "I'm having the thought that I am…" and say that to yourself ten times.

Finally, I want you to change it to "I'm noticing I'm having the thought that I am…" and repeat that to yourself ten times.

What did you notice? Was there a difference in the way those three statements felt for you? You might have noticed that the statements started to feel lighter, or more distant. You might have noticed that it started to feel less definite and as if you could have an option about whether you believed the thought or not. You might not have noticed anything different, which is fine too. I've noticed that this technique really works for some people and not for others, there are plenty more defusion techniques in ACT to explore if that's the case for you.

You might be thinking that it feels too simple to just change a few words in your mind. The challenge is consistency. To loosen the power of these 'I am' statements we need to practise noticing them when they come up and internally verbalise "I'm noticing the thought that I am…". Once we've 'loosened up' our relationship with our critical thoughts, instead of unconsciously reacting to them, we can then choose what would be most helpful to do next. This is an important part of being psychologically flexible.

Going back to my mind's 'I am fat' chat, when I'm able to notice it as a recurring thought pattern that was trying to save me from being bullied, I feel less emotional sting, less need to engage in a short-term coping strategy and more able to just get on with my day. This technique of defusion can help us create some distance and change our relationship with individual thoughts. Next, I want us to explore how we can use another distancing technique to change our relationship with our Inner Critic as a whole.

Naming Your Inner Critic

Changing the dynamics of any relationship starts with increasing our understanding of the other person. So often we trip ourselves up because of the assumptions we make about the intentions of others. It is no different in our relationship with ourselves. With our Inner Critic, we often make the unconscious assumption that this part of us isn't on our side and is out to get us. When we instead see it as a part of us that is trying to help us survive, we can start to have a greater amount of compassion for it.

Giving a group of critical thoughts we regularly experience a name enables us to see more easily that 'we are not our thoughts' and to start to create a little space between our unhelpful thoughts and the part of us that is observing these thoughts. It opens the opportunity to change our relationship with these thoughts, and therefore, ourselves. It is this shift in the quality of the relationship with ourselves that results in lasting change in our behaviours towards ourselves.

Why not have a go. What could you name your inner critic? It might be a cartoon character like Mr Burns from *The Simpsons* or Eeyore from *Winnie the Pooh*. Sometimes starting with the name can be hard, so have a think about what your Inner Critic would look like if it were a person or animal. What is it wearing? What's the expression on its face? What is its catchphrase?

As with the defusion exercise earlier, for some people, this exercise will come relatively easily and might even be enjoyable. For others it just won't resonate at all, and that's fine. The great thing about ACT is that there are lots of different ways to improve our relationship with our thoughts, which are suited to different brains.

One of my coaching clients, who the 'naming your Inner Critic' activity worked well for, was Katie. She couldn't connect to any specific name so she called hers, 'She who would not be named,' which we agreed was powerful, in a Harry Potter kind of way.

We explored how she felt about 'She who would not be named' and she spoke about her being a bitch who was very mean to her. I asked her how she normally responded to this meanness, and she described trying to ignore her and push her away. We talked about how this part of her might feel when it was ignored and pushed away, and she spoke about it being frustrated and worried. She recognised that this could make the voice get louder in her head.

I asked her what she thought 'She who would not be named' wanted for her, and she said that she thought she wanted her to be happy. We reflected on how interesting it was that the part of her that was mean to her wanted her to be happy, but this intention was being lost in the delivery of the message. I was curious about how Katie would respond to a friend who was feeling ignored and pushed away and she described that she would listen to them and give them comfort. I asked her whether she would be happy to try the compassionate approach she described for a friend with 'She who would not be named' and what she might specifically say or do the next time the mean thoughts came up. Katie said, "I would say something like, thank you for the feedback. I get that you want me to be happy. What I am choosing to do now is to take some deep breaths and then have a walk around the block."

Over time Katie became much more comfortable with her critical inner thoughts and noticed that she felt less compelled to act on what 'She who would not be named' was saying to her.

I used a similar technique with Kerry, who you met at the start of the chapter. Exploring her Inner Critic and finding ways to change her relationship with it was the most powerful part of our coaching relationship. She shared that she started to recognise it as a part of her that helps her to have empathy for others. She noticed that if she sees it as a negative it just makes it stronger. Overall, she discovered that changing her relationship with this scared part of her gave her a chance to not live in fear anymore. The worry and doubts still showed up, but they no longer held her back or pulled her mood down for extended periods of time.

What makes this approach so useful is that it encourages an understanding and acceptance of a part of us that we see as 'bad.' If we can get to a point where we no longer see that part of us as negative but instead as trying to help us (even if it does it in a painful way), we can start to have compassion for it and for ourselves. It makes our relationship with ourselves feel less like a battle. It increases our trust in ourselves and builds a greater sense of internal safety.

You can find a set of Inner Critic coaching questions using the link provided in the Resources section at the end of the book. You can use these questions with yourself or with others.

Self-Compassion

When thirty-year-old Hazel heard, "You need to be more compassionate to yourself," for the first time, she had no idea what the other person was talking about. Thirty-year-old Hazel had just been promoted, had started her masters, which involved travelling to London for lectures two nights a week, and had bought her first flat which was desperately in need of renovation. This was not the time for bubble baths and face masks. This was a time for digging deep, pushing through, for going full Billy Ocean ('When the going gets tough, the tough get going' – apologies, that's the last terrible music reference, I promise).

If, like thirty-year-old Hazel, your Inner Critic has a stranglehold on you, you too might be feeling turned off by the idea of self-compassion. I get it. It took me a LONG time to work out what self-compassion really was and how it is a strength not a weakness.

Reflect for a moment: how do you think your own Inner Critic is feeling when it's sharing its hurtful judgements with you? When I ask coaching clients how they think their Inner Critic is feeling, the most frequent response is 'scared.' Which makes sense in the context of our earlier discussion about how it's often just trying to keep us safe. Stop for a minute and think about how you would respond to a friend, colleague or a family member who is scared. The part of you that is scared needs exactly what a friend, colleague or family member would need. It needs to know that it's been heard, it needs to know that you care, and it probably needs a little comfort.

THIS for me is where self-compassion really comes into its own. Discovering the wonderful work of Kristin Neff (I highly recommend reading her book, *Self-Compassion: The Proven Power of Being Kind to Yourself*, 2011), changed my view of self-compassion and turned it into something that wasn't about 'letting myself off the hook' or being 'soft,' it turned it into a way to help me move through discomfort. Kristin has developed a three-part process that has been my go-to approach for living more easily with my Inner Critic. First, I notice and acknowledge how I am feeling. Then I notice the universal and understandable nature of feeling this way. Finally, I show myself kindness, like I would a friend.

For me, this sounds something like, "I notice that I'm feeling scared, which is perfectly understandable seeing as I'm doing a presentation to 200 people I don't know – most people would feel a little scared in that situation. It's OK though. Whatever happens I will cope with it. I will be OK."

When we catch ourselves starting to be self-critical and instead pivot to a place of self-compassion, we begin to change our relationship with ourselves. We can get that calm inner feeling that we imagine we would get if we didn't have these critical thoughts at all. The self-critical noise is still there, but we have learnt a way for it not to negatively impact us.

Like every tool I've shared with you, this one will take practice. What's great about practising self-compassion is that every time your Inner Critic pops it's head up in the future, it is an opportunity to practise. In a weird way we want the self-critical thoughts to come up so that we can get better at self-compassion. The more that we can catch ourselves and experiment with self-compassion, the more natural it will feel.

Expect it to be clunky. Expect your mind to put up a fight. When we are in a place of self-compassion we are telling our survival-focused mind that, "There is no bear." If we have a strong Inner Critic, there may be a sense of safety in feeling unsafe, if that makes sense. Saying horrible things to yourself is familiar. When we step into the discomfort of something new, even though it is a more pleasant place to be, we can feel uncomfortable. Expect that there may be some resistance and it will take some time for your mind to get used to this new relationship, to learn to trust you.

I hope that this chapter, through giving you a different perspective on your mind, and some practical ideas for how you can change your relationship with some of your uncomfortable habitual thought patterns, will enable you to live with your thoughts in a way that supports you to live a full and meaningful life.

Are You Feeling More Flexible?

That brings us to the end of the chapters on psychological flexibility. My aim with these chapters was to share some of the specific insights that have both helped me and my clients to more successfully navigate being human in a complex and confusing world.

Combining the skills from the previous three chapters, I hope you:

- Feel more able to pause, take a step back and notice what is going on around and within you,
- Have identified what matters most to you and have gained a deeper understanding of some of your uncomfortable emotions, and
- Have found a way to relate to the 'survival-focused' part of you that is fearful and critical, in a more compassionate way.

If you leave these chapters feeling less alone in the challenges you face, and more equipped to respond flexibly to the challenges that life will inevitably throw at you, then I have done my job. If I have sparked your interest and you want to know more, I have collated a list of my favourite ACT books in the Further Reading section at the end of the book.

Final Words

I once heard someone say that 'stories show us how to live.' When we read about the experiences of others, their challenges, and the way they have overcome them, we have an opportunity to take whatever's useful and integrate it into our own lives. I really hope that this book has given you something that has shown you how you can live well, particularly when life feels overwhelming.

This is also a book about supporting others, acknowledging that the way out of burnout is not alone but together. I believe wholeheartedly that change happens one conversation at a time. My hope is that by reading this book, you will feel more confident in having coaching-style conversations with others that help them to help themselves.

I also hope that this book encourages a wider conversation within organisations and teams about how we collectively cope with seemingly never-ending demands and limited resources. Time feels so short, and yet it is the time spent together, working out what is within our collective control, that is so essential. What feels such a shame is that I often work with leadership teams where people have been 'falling over' for months and the redistribution of work has increased the chance of other people in the team experiencing burnout. They come to me at the point where it almost feels too late and emergency action is needed. I'd love to see these conversations happen as more of a preventative measure, and something that is returned to on a regular basis.

In the very first chapter of this book, I spoke about endings and beginnings. As we reach the end of the book, my invitation to you is to think about what you might need to put an end to and what you would like to begin. What is the one small thing you want to take from this book and commit to putting into action? As I might say to my clients, we can have a wonderful intellectual conversation but if you don't actually do anything different then nothing is going to change (said with compassion, of course).

To help you think about what you might like to do next, here is a summary of some of the key points I covered in the book:

- The three main signs of burnout are: Overwhelming exhaustion, cynicism and detachment, and feeling ineffective.
- To prevent burnout, there are things that individuals can do AND we have to look at the con-

text they are working in, focusing on the demands they are under and the resources they have.

- Engaging in coaching-style conversations can help someone to work out what is within their control and feel empowered to start making small changes.

- We have the ability to make someone feel valued and heard just by giving them our attention and asking them some simple questions to help them to think better.

- Using a tool like the Wellbeing Wheel can be a useful starting point for re-balancing our lives and identifying small, manageable changes.

- Increasing our psychological flexibility can help us to navigate life more skilfully.

- Finding ways to step back, pause and notice, helps us to think better, giving us a better chance of making conscious choices that reflect what's important to us.

- When we have clarity about what matters most to us, we can better understand our emotional reactions and work out what our particular version of a successful and meaningful life is.

- Our minds are wired to keep us safe, and they often try to do that by giving us the gift of internal negative chatter. This chatter can distract us and can hold us back from living the life we really want to live. When we can change our relationship with our critical thoughts to a more compassionate one, we are much better able to co-exist with them in a way that enables us to do more of what matters.

Finally, it wouldn't be right if I didn't say one more thank you to my amazing clients and delegates from the NHS and Emergency Services. In this image is the name of everyone I have worked with since 2020 – It was an honour to work with you and to play a part in the incredible work you do. You continue to inspire me every day.

Acknowledgments

I want to start by saying thank you to Steve and Indie, for your patience, care and for ensuring I was fed and watered throughout the time of me writing this book. To my Mum and Dad – from one imperfect parent to another – I appreciate you giving me a start in life that encouraged both independence and the drive to make a difference to others.

A massive thank you to Helen Ives, Dan Winter-Bates, Emma Lampard and Michaela Tarrant who are champions of supporting NHS staff to do their best work and stay well. Without your belief, trust and encouragement I wouldn't have been able to do the work I do.

My coaching, training and facilitation practice evolved the way it did because of my incredible clients. Thank you so much for putting your trust in me, I've learnt so much from every single person I had the privilege to work with. A special thank you to Gavin and the clients who kindly gave me permission to share their stories in this book (you know who you are). Thank you, I am sure for many people your stories will be the most valuable part of the book.

Thank you to Nicola and the team at the Unbound Press for getting me to this point and to Dr Rachael Skews for your guidance and advice, which helped shape the final version of this book. A big thank you to Dr Joe Oliver for being such an amazing ACT mentor and for taking the time to write a beautiful foreword for this book.

Last but not least, thank you to the Open House Deli team in Winchester, where your cappuccinos, delicious porridge and excellent playlists created an environment for the writing magic to happen.

Abbreviations

ACT – Acceptance & Commitment Therapy

CBT – Cognitive Behavioural Therapy

NHS – National Health Service (UK)

RFT – Relational Frame Theory

WHO – The World Health Organisation

References

Bakker, A B, & Demerouti, E (2007). *The Job Demands-Resources Model: State of the art.* Journal of managerial psychology

Bond, F W, & Bunce, D (2000). *Mediators of Change in Emotion-Focused and Problem-Focused Worksite Stress Management Interventions.* Journal of Occupational Health Psychology, 5 (1), 156–163.

Bond, F W, & Flaxman, P E (2006). *The Ability of Psychological Flexibility and Job Control to Predict Learning, Job Performance, and Mental Health.* Journal of Organizational Behavior Management, 26 (1-2), 113–130.

Covey, S (1989). *The Seven Habits of Highly Effective People: Restoring the Character Ethic.* New York, Simon and Schuster.

Fredrickson, B (2011). *Positivity: Groundbreaking Research To Release Your Inner Optimist And Thrive.* London, One World Publications.

Fogg, B J (2020). *Tiny Habits: The small changes that change everything.* Boston, Houghton Mifflin Harcourt.

Hayes, S (2019). *A Liberated Mind: How to Pivot Toward What Matters.* New York: Avery.

Kline, N (1999). *Time to Think: Listening to Ignite the Human Mind*. Hachette, UK.

Maslach, C, & Leiter, M P (2016). *Understanding the Burnout Experience: Recent research and its implications for psychiatry*. World Psychiatry: Official Journal of the World Psychiatric Association (WPA), 15 (2), 103–111.

Nagoski, E & Nagoski, A (2019). *Burnout: The Secret to Unlocking the Stress Cycle.* New York, Ballantine Books.

Neff, K D (2011). *Self-Compassion: The proven power of being kind to yourself.* New York: William Morrow.

Madore, K P, & Wagner, A D (2019). *Multicosts of Multitasking. Cerebrum: The Dana Forum on Brain Science.* 2019, cer-04-19.

Maslach, C, & Leiter, M P (2016). *Understanding the Burnout Experience: Recent Research and Its Implications for Psychiatry.* World Psychiatry, 15, 103-111.

Monahan, M (2019). *Don't Hate, Meditate! 5 Easy Practices to Get You Through the Hard Sh*t.* Ten Speed Press.

McGonigal, K. (2015). *The Upside of Stress: Why Stress Is Good for You, and How to Get Good at It.* Avery.

Petrie, N. (2023). https://www.linkedin.com/pulse/how-avoid-burnout-2023-findings-nick-petrie-2uq0c/?trackingId=XtyNRvFBQDy7ug5AqLoCjA%3D%3D

Seligman, M E (1972). Learned Helplessness. Annual Review of Medicine, 23 (1), 407-412.

Skews, R (2018). *Acceptance and Commitment Therapy (ACT) Informed Coaching: Exam- ining Outcomes and Mechanisms of Change.* Doctoral thesis, Goldsmiths, University of London.

Spitznagel, M B, Updegraff, A S G, Was, C, Martin, J T, Sislak, M, Wiborg, L, & Twohig, M P (2022). *An Acceptance and Commitment Training Program Reduces Burden Transfer, Stress, and Burnout Among Veterinary Healthcare Teams.* Journal of the American Veterinary Medical Association, 260 (12), 1554–1561.

Szarko, Alison; Ramona, Houmanfar; Smith, Gregory; Jacobs, Negar; Smith, Brooke; Assemi, Kian; Piasecki, Melissa; Baker, Timothy (2022). *Impact of Acceptance and Commitment Training on Psychological Flexibility and Burnout in Medical Education.* Journal of Contextual Behavioral Science.

Towey-Swift, K D, Lauvrud, C, & Whittington, R (2023). *Acceptance and Commitment Therapy (ACT) for Professional Staff Burnout: A systematic review and narrative synthesis of controlled trials.* Journal of Mental Health (Abingdon, England), 32 (2), 452–464.

Whitmore, J (1992). *Coaching For Performance: A Practical Guide To Growing Your Own Skills.* London: Nicholas Brealey Publishing.

WHO: *Burnout An 'Occupational Phenomenon'*: International Classification of Diseases. Geneva: World Health Organization; 2019. Available from: https://www.who.int/news/item/28-05-2019-burn-out-an-occupational-phenomenon-international-classification-of-diseases

Resources

Support available if you are concerned about your mental health:

https://www.nhs.uk/mental-health/

https://www.mentalhealth.org.uk/explore-mental-health/get-help

https://www.mind.org.uk/

Sleep advice:

https://www.mind.org.uk/information-support/types-of-mental-health-problems/sleep-problems/tips-to-improve-your-sleep/

Bonus materials: hazelandersonturner.co.uk/bonus

- How to process emotions.
- GROW questions.
- Inner Critic coaching questions.

E-books/worksheets on my website:
https://hazelandersonturner.co.uk/resources/

- Boundaries e-book
- ACT for coaches
- Values worksheet

The Coaching UnpACT podcast:
https://hazelandersonturner.co.uk/coaching-unpact/

Further Reading

Burnout
ACT for Burnout: Recharge, Reconnect, and Transform Burnout with Acceptance and Commitment Therapy by Debbie Sorenson (Jessica Kingsley Publishers, 2024).

Burnout: The Secret to Unlocking the Stress Cycles by Emily Nagoski and Amelia Nagoski (Ballantine Books, 2020).

Acceptance & Commitment Therapy
ACTivate Your Life: An Acceptance and Commitment Therapy Workbook for Building a Life that is Rich, Fulfilling and Fun by Joe Oliver, Jon Hill and Eric Morris (Robinson, 2024).

The Happiness Trap: How to Stop Struggling and Start Living by Russ Harris (Shambhala Publications, 2008).

The Little ACT Workbook: An Introduction to Acceptance and Commitment Therapy: A mindfulness-based guide for leading a full and meaningful life by Dr Michael Sinclair and Dr Matthew Beadman (Crimson Publishing, 2018).

A Liberated Mind: The essential guide to ACT by Dr Steven Hayes (Vermilion, 2019).

Our Inner Critic
Chatter: The Voice in Our Head and How to Harness It by Ethan Kross (Vermilion, 2022).

Self-Compassion: The Proven Power of Being Kind to Yourself by Kristin Neff (William Morrow Paperbacks, 2011).

Neurodiversity

ADHD an A-Z: Figuring it Out Step by Step by Leanne Maskell (Jessica Kingsley Publishers, 2022).

Autism in Adults (Overcoming Common Problems) by Luke Beardon (Sheldon Press, 2021).

Neurodiversity Coaching: A Psychological Approach to Supporting Neurodivergent Talent and Career Potential by Nancy Doyle and Almuth McDowall (Routledge, 2023).

Emotions

Emotional Agility: Get Unstuck, Embrace Change and Thrive in Work and Life by Susan David (Penguin, 2017).

Permission to Feel: Unlocking the Power of Emotions to Help Our Kids, Ourselves and Our Society Thrive by Marc Brackett (Caladon Books, 2019).

Habit Change

Healthy Habits Suck: How to Get Off the Couch and Live a Healthy Life… Even If You Don't Want To by Danya Lee-Baggley (New Harbinger, 2019).

Tiny Habits: Why Starting Small Makes Lasting Change Easy by BJ Fogg (Virgin Books, 2020).

Overcoming Busyness

Busy: How to thrive in a world of too much by Tony Crabbe (Piatkus, 2014).

Essentialism: The Disciplined Pursuit of Less by Greg McKeown (Virgin Books, 2014).

Four Thousand Weeks: Embrace your limits. Change your life. Make your four thousand weeks count by Oliver Burkeman (Vintage, 2022).

Coaching Skills for Leaders
The Coaching Habit: Say Less, Ask More & Change the Way You Lead Forever by Michael Bungay Stanier (Box of Crayons Press, 2016).

About the Author

Hazel Anderson-Turner is a Business and Coaching Psychologist who, after experiencing burnout herself, went on a mission to support leaders and teams to increase their resilience and prevent burnout. Her experience of coaching and training within the NHS during the Covid Pandemic strengthened her use of Acceptance & Commitment Therapy within coaching. She now trains coaches worldwide in this approach and co-hosts The Coaching UnpACT Podcast.

Earlier in her career, Hazel's drive to make a difference drew her to work in Organisational and Leadership Development within the Public Sector, and later to work with the NHS and Emergency Services when she started her own consultancy.

She is known for her genuineness and her depth of knowledge, and for providing evidence-based interventions that are both relatable and engaging.

Stay in Touch

If you have any questions or would like to have a conversation about working together then you can contact Hazel through her website: **hazelandersonturner.co.uk** where you can also find out more about the range of work she does and the different ways she can support you and your organisation.